A SECOND VIEW FROM THE MOON

A SECOND VIEW *from the* MOON

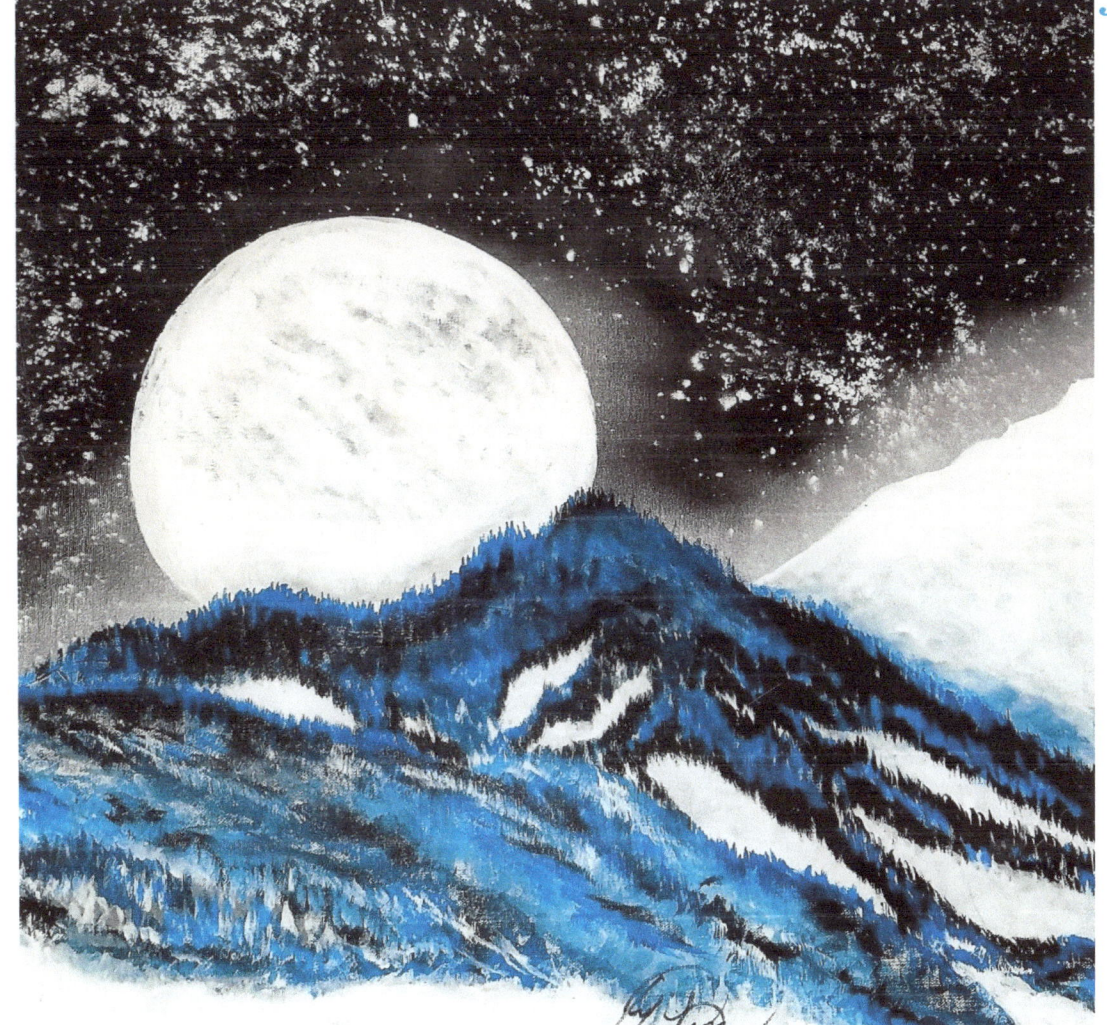

PAINTINGS

Poetry

Prose

Short Stories

TED C. LUNA

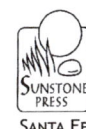

SUNSTONE
PRESS
SANTA FE

Sunstone books may be purchased for educational, business, or sales promotional use. For information please write: Special Markets Department, Sunstone Press, P.O. Box 2321, Santa Fe, New Mexico 87504-2321.

Printed on acid-free paper

∞

————————————

Library of Congress Cataloging-in-Publication Data

Names: Luna, Ted C., 1937- artist, author.
Title: A second view from the moon : paintings, poetry, prose, short
  stories / Ted C. Luna.
Description: Santa Fe : Sunstone Press, [2022]. | Summary: "Art, poetry,
  and prose from an architect in Santa Fe, New Mexico"-- Provided by
  publisher.
Identifiers: LCCN 2021050070 | ISBN 9781632933591 (paperback)
Subjects: LCSH: Luna, Ted C., 1937---Themes, motives. | Painting,
  American--21st century. | Prose poems, American--21st century. | LCGFT:
  Paintings. | Poetry. | Prose poems. | Short stories.
Classification: LCC ND237.L864 A4 2022 | DDC 720.92--dc23
LC record available at https://lccn.loc.gov/2021050070

————————————

WWW.SUNSTONEPRESS.COM

SUNSTONE PRESS / POST OFFICE BOX 2321 / SANTA FE, NM 87504-2321 /USA
(505) 988-4418

WITH L SQUARED + C
(LIKE, LOVE AND COMPANIONSHIP)
STEPHANIE, RICHARD, KRISTIN
KENNY, EMBER, ERIC, PEGGY
REGINA, CLINTON
DESTINY

MAY JOY AND HAPPINESS
BE WITH YOU FOREVER
AS IT HAS BEEN FOR ME

PROLOGUE

A VIEW FROM THE MOON WAS MY LEGACY UNTIL I REALIZED MY LEGACY WOULD CONTINUE AND I HAD SO MANY NEW WORKS TO PUBLISH. SO, I PENNED MY SECOND VIEW FROM THE MOON. EVERYTHING IS NEW AND I HOPE REFRESHING. FICTION, FANTASY, FACTS SPRINKLED WITH REAL LIFE TRUTHS AND TRAVEL. I FEEL CONFIDENT THAT YOU WILL BE ABLE TO FIGURE IT OUT FOR YOUR ENJOYMENT. WHEN I WAS JUST A PUP AND WORKING FOR AN ICON NEW MEXICO ARCHITECT, W.C. KRUGER IN SANTA FE, BOB KRUGER (NO RELATION TO W.C.) TOOK A LIKING TO ME AND HE SPENT PERSONAL TIME TEACHING ME RENDERINGS. IN THOSE DAYS IT WAS PENCIL, COLORED PENCIL OR WATERCOLOR. HE GAVE ME THIS ADVICE: "SOMEONE HAS TO START YOU AND SOMEONE HAS TO STOP YOU." THAT SOMEONE, I REALIZED, WAS ME. IT HAS GUIDED ME THOUGH LIFE IN THE CREATIVE PROCESS.

THE CREATIVE PROCESS HAS NO LIMITS. AS IN ZEN IT'S BEST BY DOING. I BELIEVE THAT ALL THINGS HAVE A SPIRIT. THE ASIAN MASTERS OF JAPAN WILL ALLOW A FLAW IN THEIR WORKS FOR THE SPIRIT TO BE RELEASED. YOU WILL NOTICE THIS IN MY WORKS IN THINGS SUCH AS SPELLING, GRAMMAR AND OMISSIONS OR COMISSIONS. SOMETIMES IT'S ACCIDENTAL OR INTENTIONAL. NO ESTEEMED EDITOR WOULD EVER ALLOW THIS. THE WORLD IS FULL OF PERFECTIONISTS. JUST LIKE YOUR COMPUTER WORKS (NO MISTAKES) BEFORE YOU CONTINUE.

MY PROSE NOVEL LANCE AND LAURA WAS AN ADDITION JUST BECAUSE I SHOULD WRITE ONE. THEIR ADVENTURES ARE IN PLACES THAT I HAVE BEEN TO AND ARE REAL, OF COURSE, WITH SOME POETIC LICENSE. I HOPE TO CONTINUE THEIR ADVENTURES IN THE NEXT BOOK. THE PAINTINGS, POETRY, PHOTOS, PROSE AND SKETCHES ARE ALL NEW. I GUESS MY FANTASIES ARE MORE FUN AND GETTING BETTER. AS YOU KNOW, I SOMETIMES TWIST THE FACTS.

OUR WORLD IS BEAUTIFUL AND MOST OF THE HUMAN POPULATION IS KIND AND CONSIDERATE, IF ONLY YOU TRAVEL IT WITH AN OPEN AND KIND ATTITUDE. TROUBLED AREAS ARE JUST PEOPLE TRYING TO HAVE A BETTER LIFE AND DOING SOMETHING ABOUT IT.

DREAM AN ADVENTURE TO SOME PLACE YOU HAVE NEVER BEEN.
MAKE IT A REALITY, GO FOR IT. IT WILL ALWAYS BE A MEMORY
IN THE THEATER OF THE MIND.

TED C. LUNA

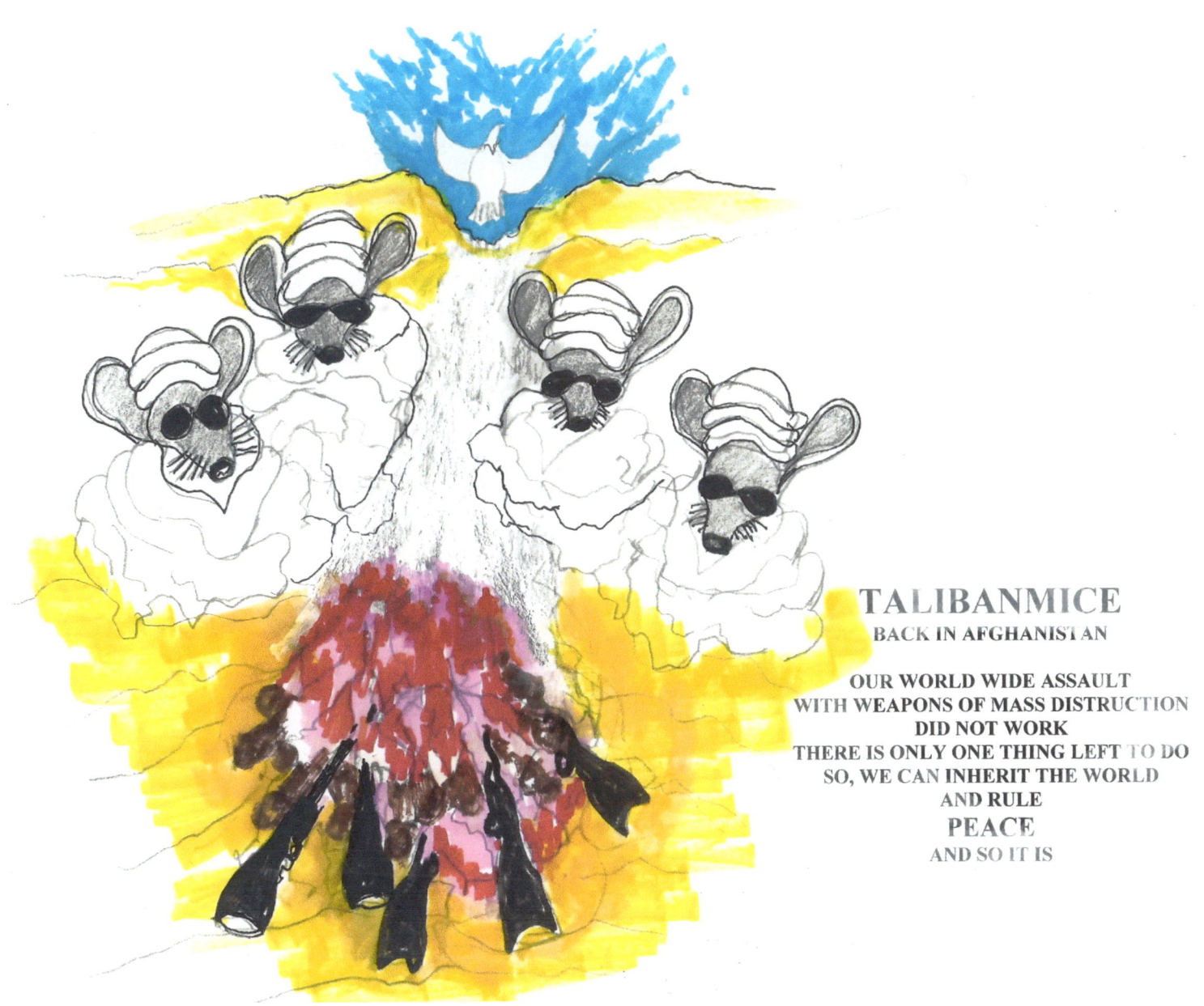

TALIBANMICE
BACK IN AFGHANISTAN

OUR WORLD WIDE ASSAULT
WITH WEAPONS OF MASS DISTRUCTION
DID NOT WORK
THERE IS ONLY ONE THING LEFT TO DO
SO, WE CAN INHERIT THE WORLD
AND RULE
PEACE
AND SO IT IS

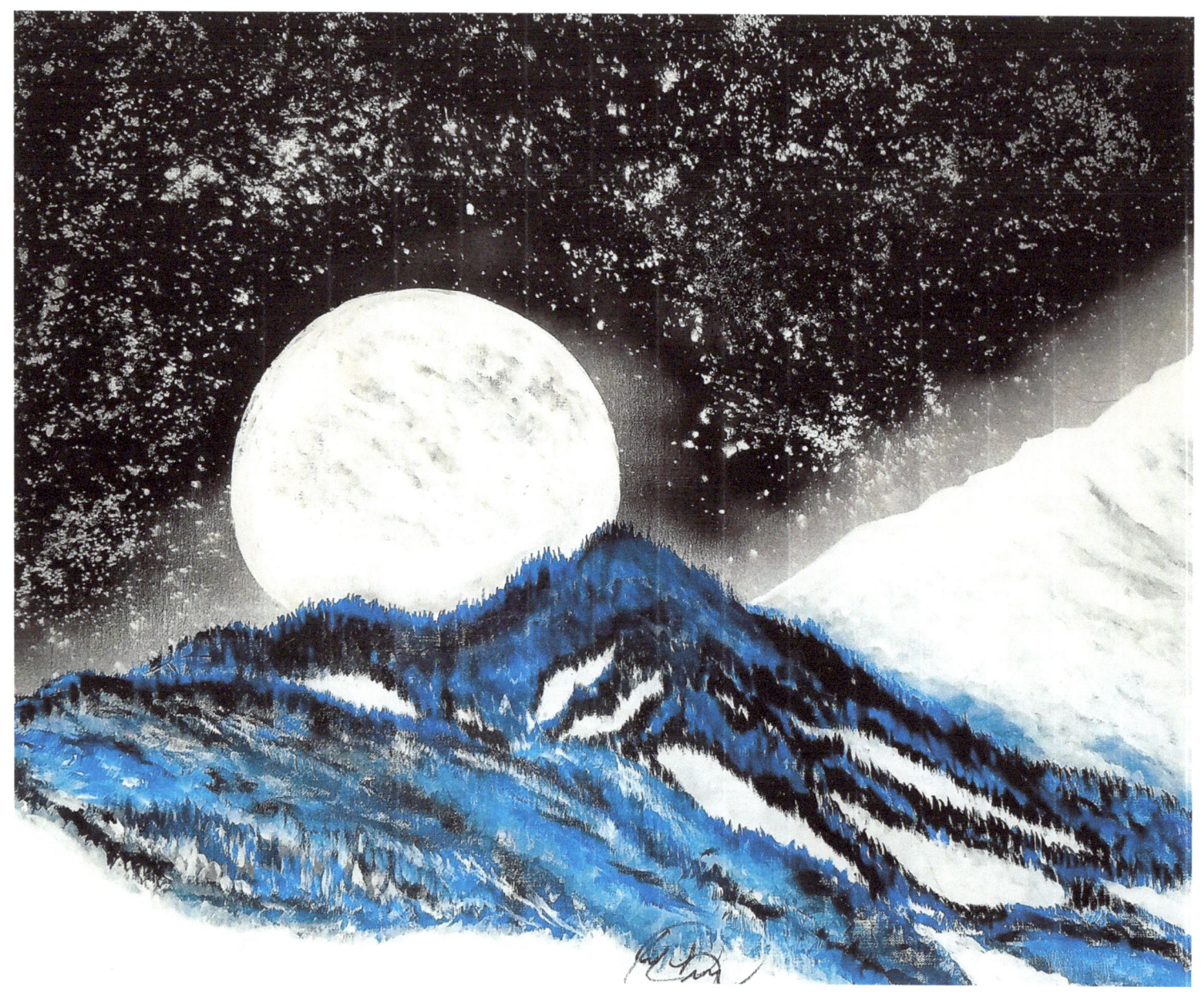

10

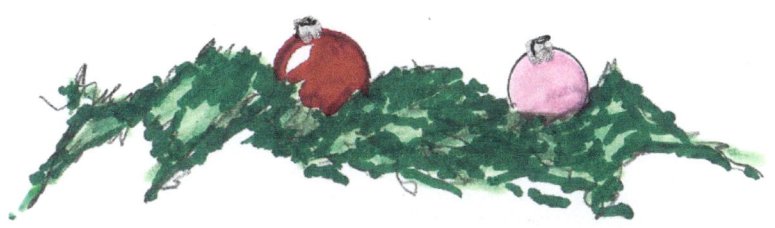

SANTA

FLAPJACKS BURNT BACON MAPLE SYRUP TOO
EARLY MORNING AT THE KITCHEN TABLE
IT HAS SNOWED LAST NIGHT A FOOT OR TWO
MY DAUGHTER LOOKED AT ME
WITH A TWINKLE IN HER BLUE EYES
DAD SHE ASKED CAN WE GO OUT AND PLAY
MOM WILL SIT AT THE FIREPLACE ALL DAY

THE SUNLIGHT IS BRIGHT IN WONDERFUL DAY
GET DRESSED IN YOUR SNOW WEATHER GEAR
DON'T FORGET THE GOGGLES OR SNOW BOOTS
I'LL DO THE SAME MEET ME OUTSIDE
THEN WE WILL CLIMB THE HILL
FIRST, I'LL GET THE RED FLYER
THAT HUNG IN THE GARAGE WALL
I BOUGHT FOR HER A YEAR AGO

A BEAUTIFUL RED SLED WITH HANDLE BARS
WITH A SMALL NYLON ROPE
TO TOW IT UP HILL, WAXED THE RUNNERS
I MET HER OUTSIDE WE ARE READY TO GO
AT THE TOP OF THE HILL DON'T MAKE
GOGGLE EYES AT JOHNNY HE WILL
NOT KNOW WHAT TO DO BUT RACE
TO BE FIRST AT THE BOTTOM OF THE HILL

FOUND A SPOT UNDER A TREE
OF COURSE, IT WAS
AT THE BOTTOM OF THE HILL
I COULD NOT COUNT HER RUNS
BUT ON HER LAST SHE CRASHED
HIGH SHOUTS LAUGHING
WITH HER MOUTH FULL OF SNOW
HEY SWEETHEART ITS TIME TO GO

IN THE HOUSE WE WENT SET BY
THE FIREPLACE DRINKING APPLE CIDER
I SPIKED MINE WITH OLD CROW
IT'S CHRISTMAS EVE MAKE SURE
THE FIRE IS OUT LEAVE TREATS
FOR SANTA AND THE RAINDEER
I KNEW THEN WHAT I MUST DO

AFTER DINNER ABOUT TWILIGHT
I READY THE TREATS AS SHE WATCHED ME
ARRANGE THINGS ON THE FIREPLACE TABLE
DAD SHE SAID NO MILK AND COOKIES
I POURED A GLASS OF KNOB HILL
AND A BOTTLE OF BURGANDY WINE
A BAG OF LAYS PATATOE CHIPS
THIS WILL INSURE THAT
SANTA WILL KNOW YOU HAVE BEEN NICE GIRL
DARLING GO TO BED ITS BEEN A LONG DAY

THE BEST OF SWEET DREAMS
WITH A GOOD NIGHT KISS
TOMORROW MORNING WILL BE
FULL OF SURPRISES UNDER THE TREE
ANGELS SING AND DANCE
AS YOU ARE ONE TO MOM AND ME

THEODORO CORONA LUNA

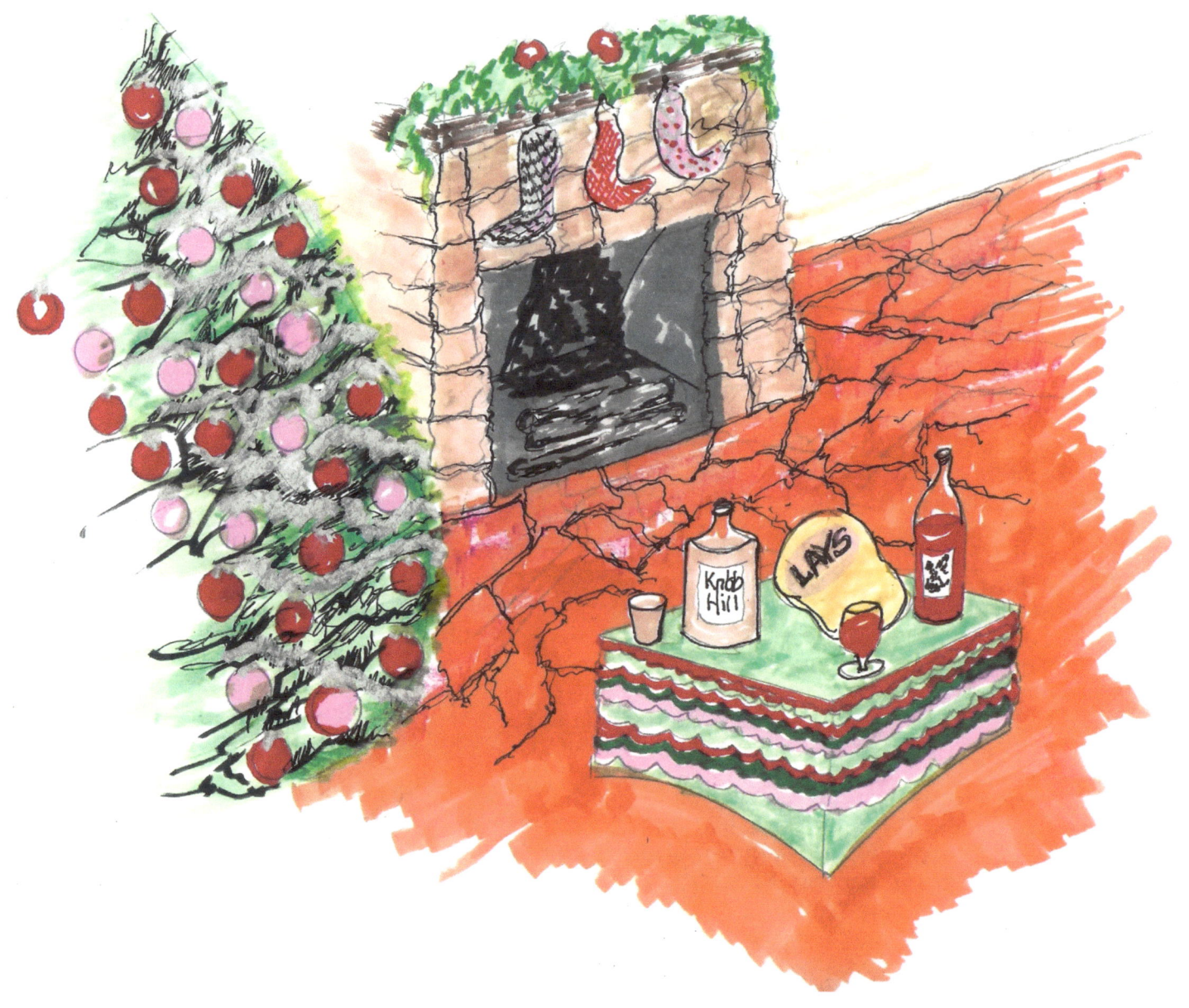

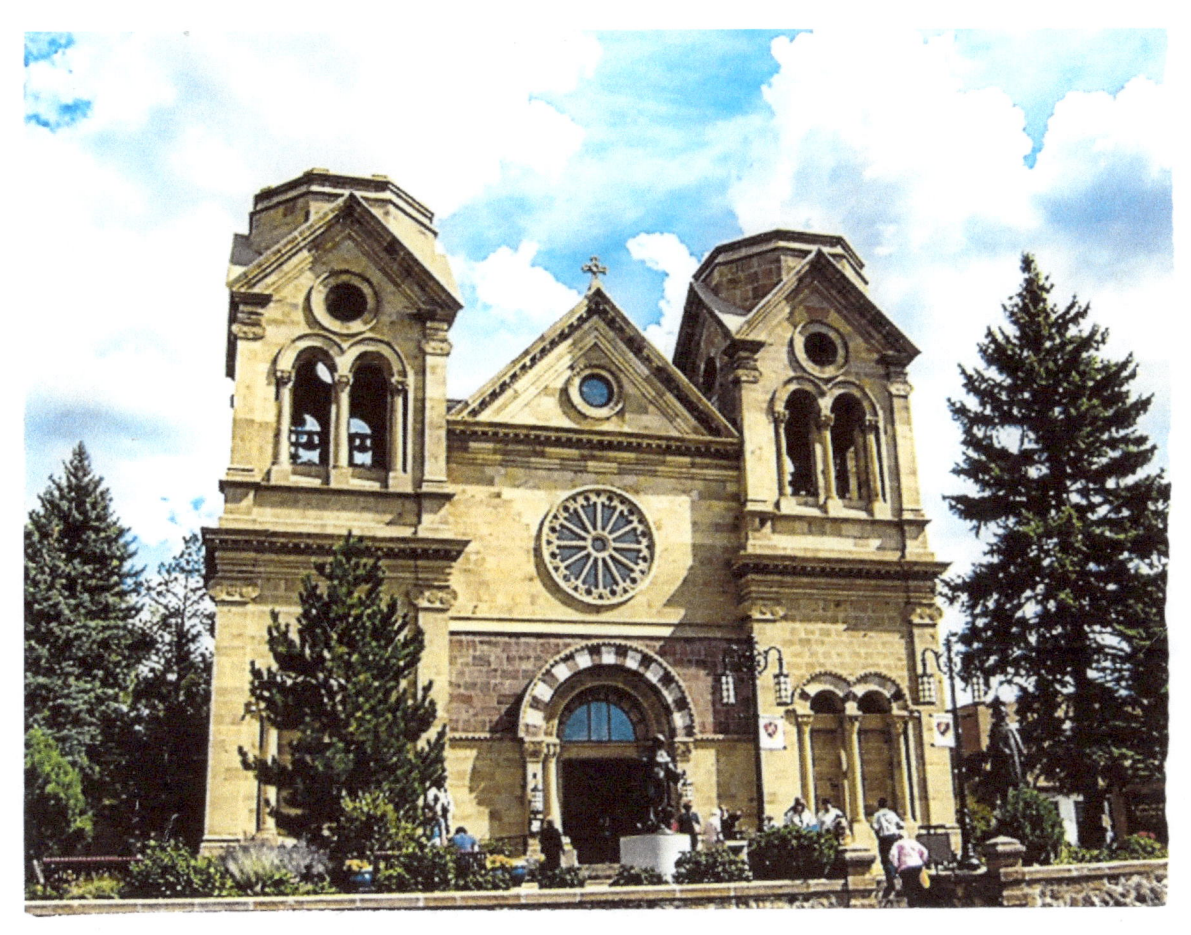

SAINT FRANCIS
CATHEDRAL
BASILICA OF ST. FRANCIS
OF ASSISI IN SANTA FE

IN LATE SUMMER I MOVED MY
FAMILY BACK TO SANTA FE
I WAS HIRED BY URBAN WEIDNER
AWAITING THE RESULTS OF MY
4 DAY EXAMS TO BE ORDAINED
A REGISTERED ARCHITECT

URBANS OFFICE WAS IN A BUILDING
THAT HOUSED KTRC RADIO STATION
THE SANTA FE NEW MEXICAN NEWSPAPER
THE RADIO STEEL TOWER STILL STANDS
A FEW YEARS LATER I WOULD
HAVE MY THIRD OFFICE ACROSS
THIS BUILDING ON MARCY STREET

HE WAS ASKED TO DO A NEW ROOF
ON THE CATHEDRAL HE INCLUDED ME
TO DO THE SITE WORK AND ALL
OF THE CONTRACT DOCUMENTS FOR
NORMAL BIDDING AND CONTRACTOR
SELECTION, THE PROCESS WENT WELL

URBAN HAD THE CONTRACT
TO DO MOST OF THE WORK
FOR THE ARCHDIOCESE OF SANTA FE
HE WAS A DEVOUT CATHOLIC WITH
14 CHILDEREN AND PRETTY WIFE
THEIR HOME WAS ON ARROYO CHAMISA

THE REMOVAL OF THE EXISTING ROOF
MATERIAL WAS FAST THE DECKING
WAS GOOD FOR THE NEW ROOFING
THE ROOFER CALLED US AND ASKED
US FOR A FAST-ON-SITE INSPECTION
WE WERE AMAZED AT THE DISCOVERY

IN ORDER TO KEEP BOTH, THE
RIDGE AND EAVES STRIAGHT
AS VIEW FROM THE GROUND LEVEL
WE INSTRUCTED THE ROOFER
HOW TO SEAL AND KEEP
THIS AREA TRIANGULAR FLAT

AT THE RIDGE LINE OF THE ROOF
THERE WAS A TRIANGULAR FLAT
AREA THAT WAS 24" WIDE AT THE
HIGH EAST WALL OF THE ALTAR
THE YELLOW LIME STONE WALLS
THE NORTH AND SOUTH
WERE 24" OUT OF LINE

TO THIS DAY THE ROOF REMAINS
THE ROMANESQUE REVIVAL
CATHEDRAL ORIGINALLY WAS
DESIGNED TO HAVE 160' STEEPLES
AT THE WEST ENTRY TOWERS
THEY RAN OUT OF FUNDS
IN A WAY IT RESEMBLES
NOTRE DAMN IN FRANCE

A FEW MONTHS LATER
I WAS ORDAINED A
REGISTERED ARCHITECT
MY STOREYS AS ALWAYS
WILL CONTINUE

THEODORO CORONA LUNA

VORTEX

I KNOW IT IS REAL AND I'LL TELL YOU SO
SEATING ON THE BROW OF THE HILL
TAKING IN THE MOUNTAINS AND VALLEY
BELOW WATER GRASS FIELDS SPARKLED
WITH DROPS OF DIAMONDS CAUSED BY THE SUN
AT PEACE WITH BEING
ALLTHIS BEAUTY TO BE HOLD
WITH OPEN MIND I CLOSED MY EYES

I FELT THIS VORTEX OF ENERGY
SAIL STRIGHT THRU TO MY SPIRIT
NOT TO SOUL IT DOES NOT EXIST
COSMIC RAYS WITH INVISABLE LIGHT
IT DID NOT LAST LONG
WHAT COULD BE
IT CHANGED MY VIEW OF LIFE
REALITY WAS BRAND NEW

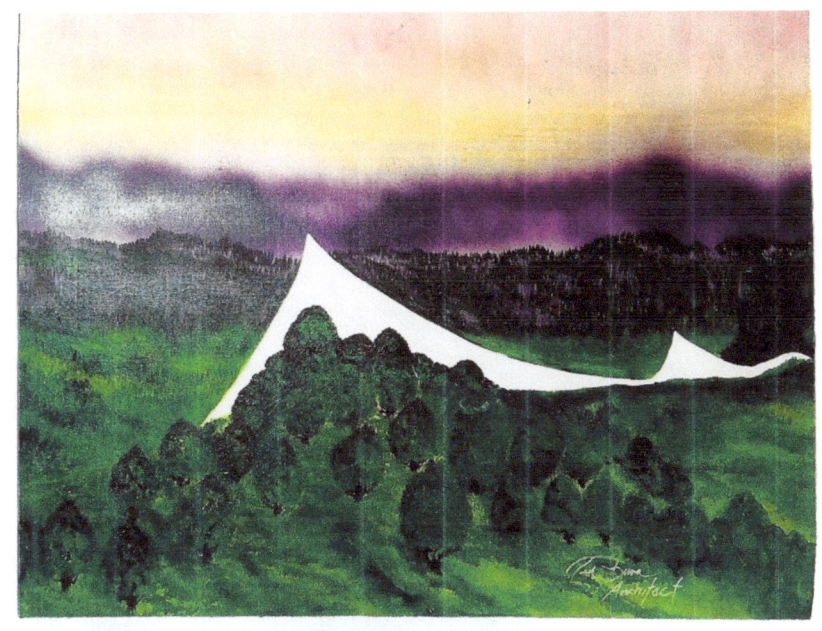

SCIENCE IN MY MIND
TRIED TO EXPLAIN
COLLESION OF MAGNETIC FIELDS
ENERGEY RAYS FROM ABOVE
OR ANCIENT SPIRITS BOUND IN THE EARTH
NATIVE AMERICANS HAD SACRED PLACES
EVEN TODAY ALL VISTORS STAY AWAY
FOR THEY NEW VORTEX

ANGEL FIRE, NM IS WHERE THE CHAPEL TO BE
WITH RED ROCK MONOLITHS
SODONA ARIZONA I CLOSED MY EYES
SAMETHING HAPPEDED TO ME
BLESSED WITH NEW INSIGHT
WHY HAVE THE GODS CHOOSING ME?

IN STUDY OF MOTHER/FATHER EARTH
FAR AND WIDE VOTEX PLACES
ABOUND ONLY IF YOU SEE
SO, OPEN YOUR MIND CLOSE YOUR EYES
I HOPE THIS WILL HAPPEN TO YOU
AS IT HAPPENED TO ME

HOWARD AND HIS GUITAR
"IF I STARTED RUNNIN NOW
I COULD ALMOST RUN ALL THE WAY
UP THOSE PEARLY SLOPES
TO HEAVEN WHERE THEY SAY
YOU LIVE IN PERFECT PEACE
YOUR BROKEN BODY NOW RENEWED
IF I STARTED RUNNIN NOW
PRETTY SOON I'D FIND MY WAY TO YOU

YOU LEFT US WAY TO EARLY
TO GO AND FIGHT FOR ME
IN A LAND TOO FAR AWAY
ACROSS THE ROLLING SEA
BUT I ALWAYS THOUGHT THAT
YOU'D RETURN SOME DAY TO ME
BUT IN THE END, YOU
GAVE YOUR LIFE
JUST TO KEEP
OUR COUNTRY FREE

IT'S A MONUMENTAL FEELING
THAT MOVES A MAN TO WRITE
ABOUT THAT ASIAN WAR
NOT JUDGING WRONG OR RIGHT
BUT I WILL NOT FORGET YOU
OR WHY YOU FOUGHT THE FIGHT
AND YOUR MEMORY WILL ALWAYS TOUCH ME
WHEN THE MOON COMES UP BEHIND
THIS PLACE TONIGHT

THIS CHORUS REPEATS ONLY ONCE

BEST OF THE BEST
NEW MEXICO'S BALLADEER EXTRAORDINAR
HOWARD STANSELL

RUNNIN
IF I STARTED RUNNIN NOW

INTRODUCTION BY HOWARD
"I'D LIKE TO SAY THANKS TO TED LUNA
WHO INSPIRED THIS SONG? I WROTE IT
ABOUT THE VIETNAM NATIONAL
MEMORIAL IN ANGEL FIRE, NM
TED DESIGNED THE CHAPEL THERE
AND BUILT BY THE LATE DOCTOR
VICTOR WESTPALL IN MEMORY
OF HIS SON DAVID WHO HE LOST
IN THAT ASIAN WAR. AND A
SPECIAL THANKS TO DAVA ANSELL
WHO FAITHFULLY SERVED AS
THE DIRECTOR OF THE
MEMORIAL FOR SO LONG.
IT'S MY TRIBUTE TO A BUILDING
AND THOSE WHO REMEMBER
HOWARD STANSELL

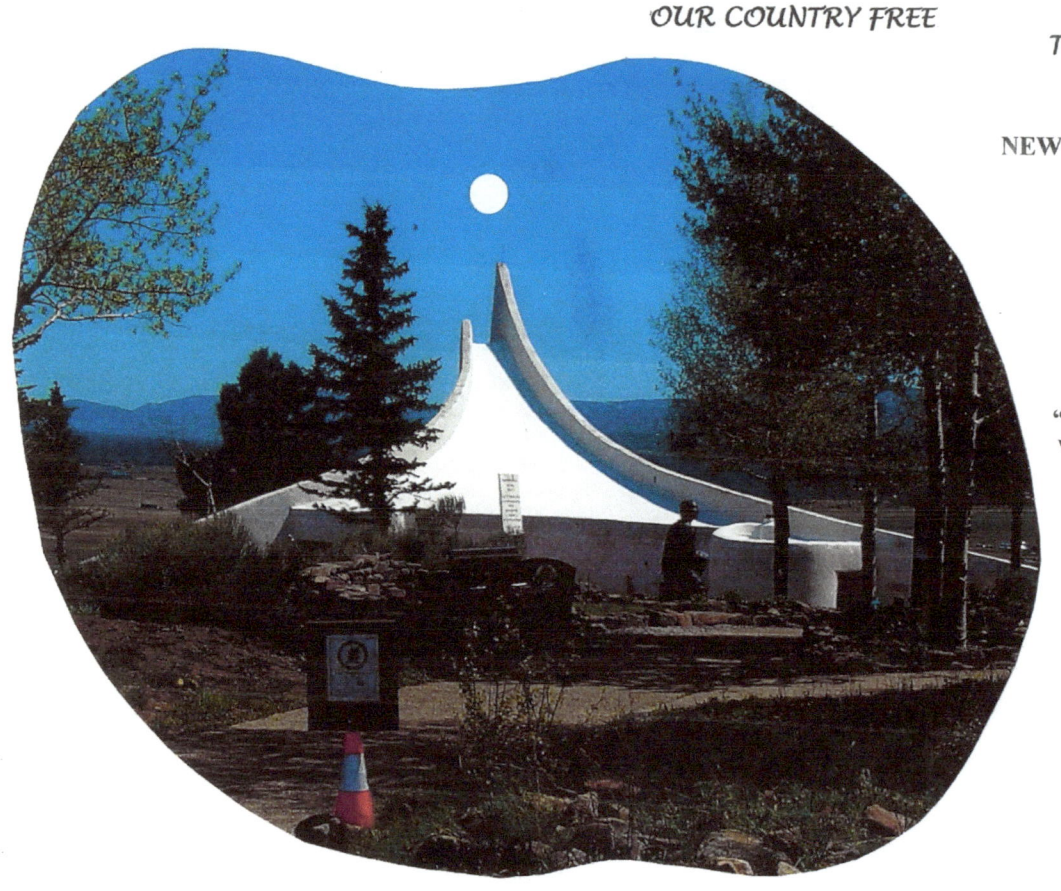

16

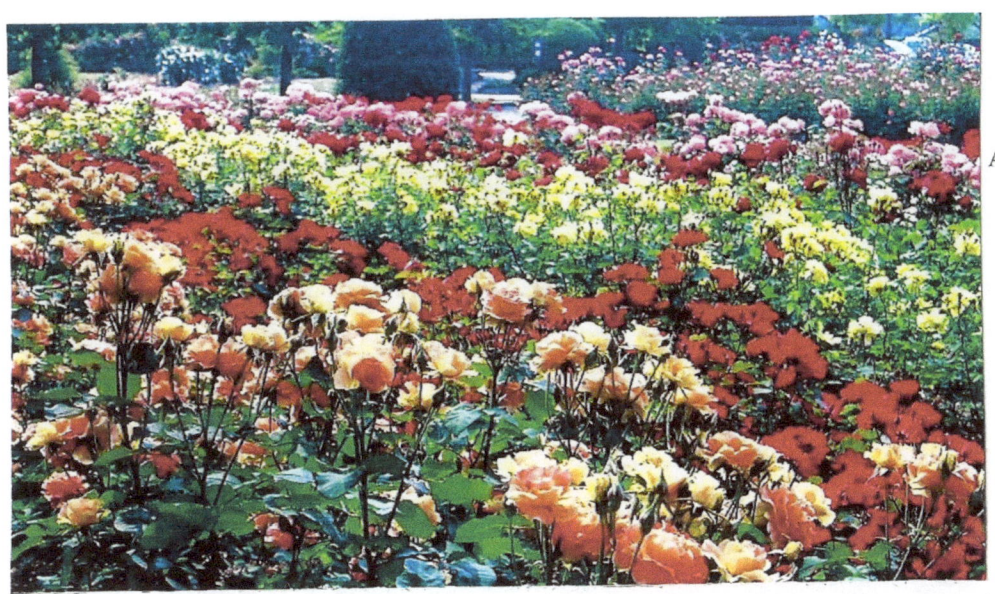

ROSE GARDEN

"I NEVER PROMISSED YOU A"
VETERANS DAY AT THE CHAPEL

THE FLY OVER BY THE FIGHTER JETS
IN MISSING MAN FORMATION
MUSIC BY THE ANGEL FIRE HIGH SCHOOL
BAND SITTING ON THE GRASS
VETERANS, FAMILIES, FROM ALL OVER
NEW MEXICO AND NEIGHBORING STATES

COLORS POSTED IN A MILITARY WAY
CLEAR BLUE SKY AND WARM SUN
AT 11 AM THE CELEBRATION BEGAN
INVOCATION AND SILENCE
DAVA AND I SITTING ON THE STAGE
THE GIFTED SPEAKERS BEGAN

HALF WAY THROUGH THE PROGRAM
A COUPLE APPREARED AND RUSHED
DIRECTLY TO THE STAGE
SHE GRABED THE MICROPHONE
FACED THE AUDIENCE AND IN
ACAPELLA SANG THE SONG

CHEERS AND CLAPPING WAS A ROAR
LIN ANDERSON BOWED AND TALKED
WITH FINAL BENEDICTION
DAVA AND I INTRODUCED OURSELVES
WARM AND FRIENDLY HAND SHAKES
SHE SAID SHE LIVED IN TAOS

SHE INVITED US TO VIST
AT HER HOME ON KIT CARSON ROAD
BEFORE SHE LEFT, I ASK HER
IF COULD WRITE A SONG ABOUT
MY CONCEPT "IF I STARTED RUNNING NOW"
THE CHAPEL WALLS INSPIRED ME

SHE SAID SHE WOULD CONSIDER IT
GIVING US HER ADDRESS AND PHONE
AND AWAY HER AND HER COMPANON WENT
WE ALL THEN WENT TO ZEBADIOUS
TO HAVE LUNCH
GREAT DAY IN ANGEL FIRES WAY

A FEW WEEKS LATER WENT TO TAOS
DAVA AND I ALWAYS LOOKING
TO FIND FUNDS FOR MEMORIAL SUPPORT
LOVELY COMFORTABLE HOME
WELLCOMING WITH TWO BEERS

AND SITTING ON THE SOFA
WE ASKED HER IF SHE COULD DO
AN ENDOWMENT FOR THE CHAPEL
SHE SAID SHE WOULD CONSIDER IT
LITTLE DID WE KNOW THAT
LIN WAS JUST ONE STEP
ABOVE PROVERTY LEVEL

WE NEVER HEARD FROM HER AGAIN
THE NEWS WE RECEIVED WE
COULD NOT BELIEVE
LIN WAS ARRESTED FOR
SHOPLIFTING AT WALMART
MORE THAN ONCE

SHE DIED A FEW YEARS LATER
WHERE SHE LIES, I DO NOT KNOW
NO MEDIA NEWS OR ANY THING ELSE
A WONDERFUL COUNTRY SINGER
LAID TO REST BUT WHERE?
I AM PROUD TO KNOWN HER

IT'S A VERY SAD STORY
BUT BELIEVE ME IT'S TRUE

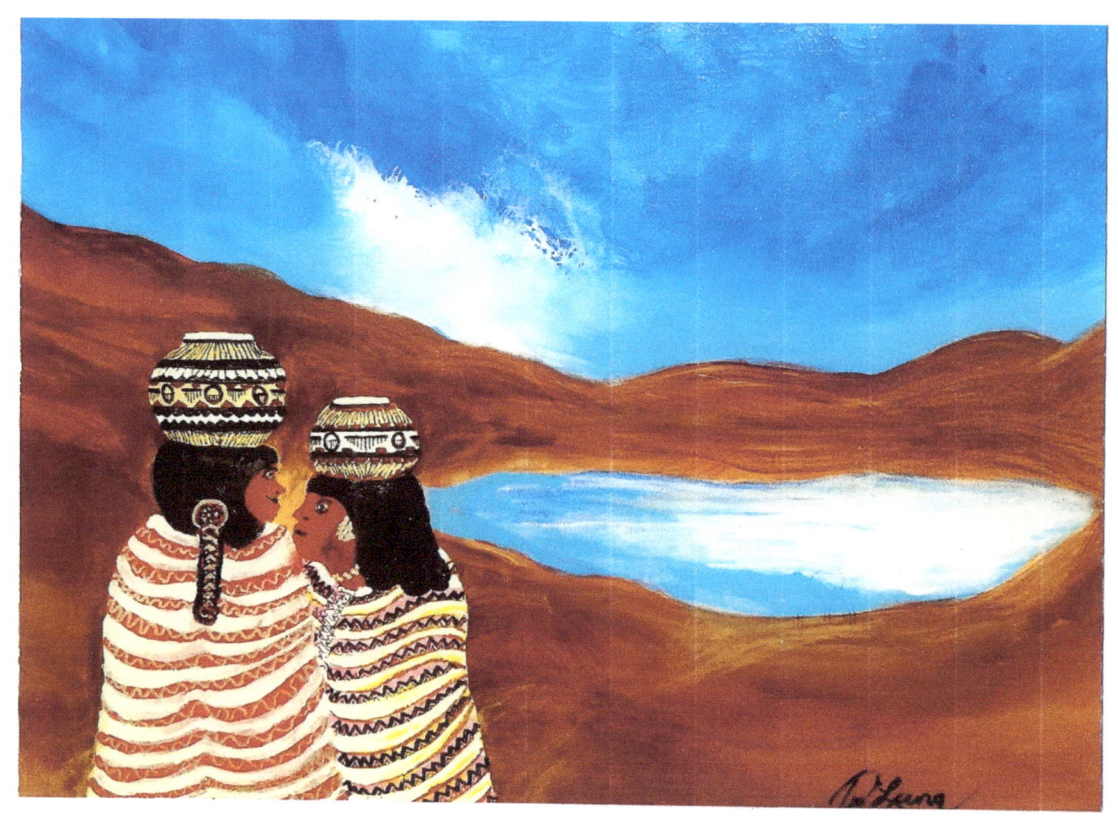

SKY CITY WATER DEPARTMENT

ACOMA PUEBLO SITS HIGH ATOP A NATURAL OUTCROPING OF SANDSTONE MONOLITH
WITH VERY STEEP SIDES MOSTLY INPOSSIBLE TO CLIMB. A MAJOR DEFENSE FOR EARLY
WARRING NATIVE NATIONS. ACESSABLE BY VERY SMALL ONE-MAN TRAILS, AND
EASELY DEFENDED. THE NATIVES CREATED ONE OF THE MOST BEAUTIFUL INDIGENOUS
NATURAL ARCHITECTURE THAT IS STILL OCCUPIED TODAY. THE VALLEY BELOW IS
WHERE THE THEY HAD WATER THUS IT WAS NATURAL FOR FARMING TO BEGAN.
WITH OCCASSIONAL RAINS THE NATURAL DEPRESSION IN AROUND THE HILL TOP
VILLAGE WOULD CATCH RAIN WATER AND EASLY GATHERED AND STORED. THIS SWEET
WATER WAS GATHERED MOSTLY BY WOMEN AND CHILDREN.
LOOKING UP FROM THE VALLEY AT THE PUEBLO WITH THE
BLUE SKY SOROUNDING IT IS TRULY SKY CITY:

LANCELOT
THE BEGANING

MOM SCREAMED IN JOY
DAD HAD TEARS RUNNING
TO THE BEARD ON HIS CHIN
IT'S A BOY THE DOCTOR SAID
I ENTERED THE WORLD
HE IS BEAUTIFUL
HIS FEATURES WILL CHANGE

I HAVE TO FILL OUT THE BIRTH
CERTIFICATE THE DOCTOR
WITH PEN IN WASHED HAND
MERRY Q. SCOTT MOTHER
WHAT DOES THE Q. STAND FOR?
EARL MY DAD SAID QUEEN

O THE DOCTOR STARTLED
LIKE MARY QUEEN OF SCOTTLAND
JUST FORGET THE OF
EARL STARTED TO LAUGH
WILL HE BE AN KNIGHT?
ONLY AT OUR SQUARE KITCHEN TABLE

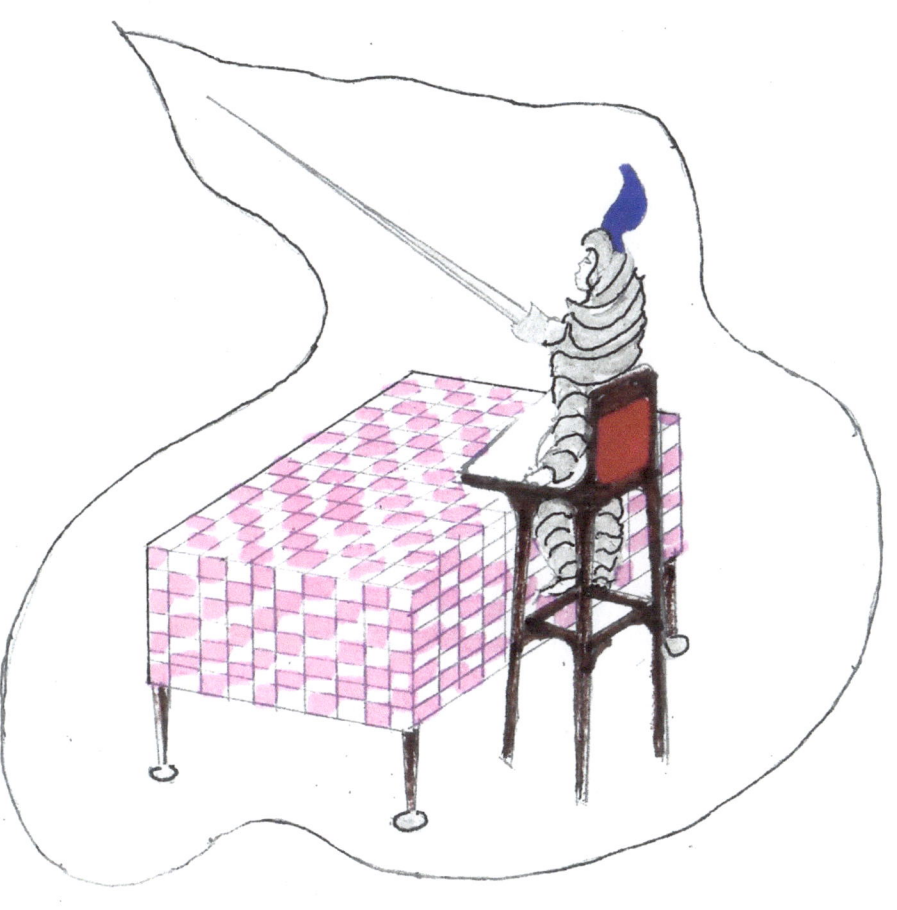

HE WILL BE CHARGED
WITH THE SAFETY OF THE KITCHEN
TO ENSURE THAT NO EVIL KNIGHTS
WOULD SWIPE THE RED AND WHITE
CHECKER BOARD PATTERN TABLE CLOTH
TALL ORDER FOR AN INFANT

THE DOCTOR THEN ASKED
WHAT ARE YOU GOING TO NAME HIM?
MERRY AND I DECIDED ON
LANCELOT, BUT HE WILL BE KNOW
LANCE SCOTT IF IT WAS A BOY
WHAT NO MIDDLE INTIAL
JUST USE E AS IN EARL

LA NCE
THE TODDLER YEARS

I WAS WEENED FROM MOM
SHE GAVE ME BABY FOOD CAME IN A CAN
SOON I WAS EATING CHOPPED UP TABLE FOOD
MY HAIR WAS BLOND ALMOST YELLOW
MY EYES TURNED TO GREEN
I COULD USE THE TOILET WITH A STOOL

THE BABY TALK WAS GONE
I LOVED THE NEW WORDS LEARNED EVERY DAY
CRAWELING LEFT BEHIND
DIAPERS LONG GONE
EXPLORING THE HOUSE AND YARD BEHIND
MOM WOULD SHOUT TO FIND ME

THE YARD HAD TREES
THAT TOLD THE SEASONS STORIES
UP I WENT TO THE LOWER BRANCH
MOM FOUND ME HANGING THERE
WITH TEARS IN HER EYES
SHOUTING "NEVER, NEVER CLIMB A TREE"

MY YEARS PAST TO FAST
EXCEPT FOR BIRTHDAYS THE REWARD
WITH CAKE AND ICE CREAM
CANDLES TO BLOW OUT
PRETTY PRESENTS TO UNWRAP
YOUR READY FOR KINDERGARDEN

WHAT KINDERGARDEN I DID ASK
A KIND LADYS HOUSE TO PLAY
AND MAKE NEW FRIENDS
WILL THERE BE GIRLS THERE
I'M SURE AND BE NICE
DEAR ITS LESS THAN A YEAR

IT WAS SHORT A FEW MONTHSF RELEIF WAS INSIGHT
GRADUATION CAME PARENTS TO ATTEND
GIVEN TREATS AND A RIBBON WITH BADGE
WITH THE WORDING I'LL FORGET
"I MADE IT THOUGH KINDERGARDEN"

LANCE
ELEMENTARY SCHOOL

MOM DO I HAVE TO GO I ASKED
YES, YOU DO THERE ARE THINGS TO LEARN
AND MOST OF THE "K" CROWED WILL BE THERE
IT WILL BE A LONG DAY EACH WEEK
THEY WILL GIVE YOU BREAKFAST
AND A NOON LUNCH

YOU CAN WALK FROM HOME TO GET THERE
DON'T TALK BUT RUN FROM STRANGERS
GO WITH YOUR NEIGHBOR NEXT DOOR
BUT MOM SHES A GIRL
BUT SHES KIND OF CUTE
YOU WILL PROTECT EACH OTHER

I HOPE SHE BE IN MY SAME CLASSROOM
TWENTY-ONE STUDENTS AS THE LAW STATED IT
A SILVER HAIRED LADY BIG AS A BOAT
KIND LOVING SMILE FROM EAR TO EAR
LITTLE DID I OR ANY ONE KNOW IT
SHE ALWAYS WAS NAMED TEACHER OF THE YEAR

READING, WRITING AND ARTHIMATIC
LATER I LEARNED IT WAS THE SAME OLD STOREY
MOM HAD TAUGHT ME HOW TO READ
COUNTLESS NIGHTS IN BED
WITH A NEVER-ENDING SUPPLY OF BOOKS
ALWAYS IN FANTASY OR FACT

MISS APRIL THUNDER TAUGHT US WELL
WHEN A DISTURBANCE IN CLASS
SHE WOULD RISE HER VOICE
FOR ALL OF US IT SOUNDED LIKE THUNDER
WE ALL KNEW HER LAST NAME WELL
THE SCHOOL YEAR ENDED,
SUMMER REST WAS HERE

ONE DOWN FIVE MORE TO GO
HOPE NEXT YEAR NO THUNDER WOULD I HEAR
SUMMER WENT TO AUTUMN
BACK TO SCHOOL I MUST GO
MOM PREPAID MY MEAL TICKETS
THE GINGLE IN MY POCKET WERE FOR TREATS

THE FIVE WENT FAST
MORE LIKE A FLASH OF LIGHTING
I HAD LEARENED EVERY THING
SO, THEY TOLD ME I WAS FREE TO GO
MIDDLE SCHOOL
"O FOR HEAVENS SAKE HERE I GO AGAIN"

LANCE
MIDDLE SCHOOL

SEVEN TO NINE WAS MY JAIL TIME
I HAD GROWEN TALL 5'5"
I TIPED THE SCALES AT 125
FIRST DAY THEY ASKED ME
DO YOU LIKE SPORTS
WOULD YOU TELL ME HER NAME AGAIN?

I WOULD SHUDDLE EVERY HOUR
TO A DIFFENT CLASS AND TEACHER
ONE WAS TO HOME ECONMICS
WHERE I LEARNED TO COOK
BAKE AND LAUNDRY CLEAN
LITTLE DID KNOW ITS MEANING
IN LATER LIFE IT WOULD SET ME FREE

THE SPORTS COACH WAS MY MATH
TEACHER AND HE ASKED TO
MEET HIM AFTER SCHOOL
HE NEEDED A QUARTER BACK
TO RUN THE FOOTBALL SHOW
HE SAID I'LL TEACH
YOU WHAT YOU NEED TO KNOW

YOUR SMART HEALTHY AND STRONG
THIS YEAR YOU WILL BACKUP
TO ALEX SINCE HE WILL GOING
HIGH SCHOOL IN MAY
NEXT YEAR YOU WILL BE
NUMBER ONE, WOW I SAID

ALL THE CLASSES SEEMED TO BE
HIGHER LEVELS OF WHAT
I LEARNED IN MIDDLE SCHOOL
THE EIGHT AND NINETH YEARS
I LEAD OUR TEAM TO WIN
THE CITY CHAMPIONSHIP

THE GIRLS SEEMED TO BLOSSOM
MY FINAL GRADES WERE HIGH
IT WAS GRADUATION TIME
MOM AND DAD WERE ESTADIC
THEY GAVE ME A 35M CANON CAMERA
WITH ROLLS OF FILM AND LENSES

TENTH, ELEVEN AND TWELVE
THE YEARS OF MY NEW JAIL SENTENCE
I SPENT THE SUMMER TAKING
ALL OF THE IMAGES OF EVERYTHING
IT BECAME APPARENT THAT THESE
WERE FROZEN MOMENTS IN TIME

DEVELOPING THE FILMS AT THE LAB
BROKE MY BUDGET FOR THE SUMMER
I HAD A SLIDE PROJECTOR
STILL HAD TO GO TO THE LAB
FOR FAVORATE IMAGES TO BE PRINTED
MOMS WORDS TO ME "NEVER CLIMB A TREE"

LANCE
HIGH SCHOOL

THE FALL YEAR CAME AND SO BE IT
THEY SAW ME PLAY IN MIDDLE SCHOOL
FIRST DAY ON THE FIELD
RUNNING A FEW LAPS THEN TO SCRIMAGE
ALL THE TEAM WAS OLDER AND BIGGER
TWO HIT ME SO HARD I RAN FROM THE FIELD

HIGH SCHOOL FOOTBALL WAS NOT FOR ME
THE CLASSES WERE DIFFERENT
THANK GOD IT WAS A BLESSING TO ME
I STUDYED HARD KEPT THE GIRLS FREE
A FEW CAUGHT MY EYE BUT NOT MY HEART
I ALLWAYS KEPT MY CAMERA WITH ME

SONIC SPEED THE YEARS WENT BY
IT WAS SOON GRADUATION TIME
I APPLIED TO BEST UNIVERSITYS
A FEW STATED THEY WOULD LET ME IN FOR FREE
MY HEART WAS SET ON HARVARD
IT WAS MENT TO BE

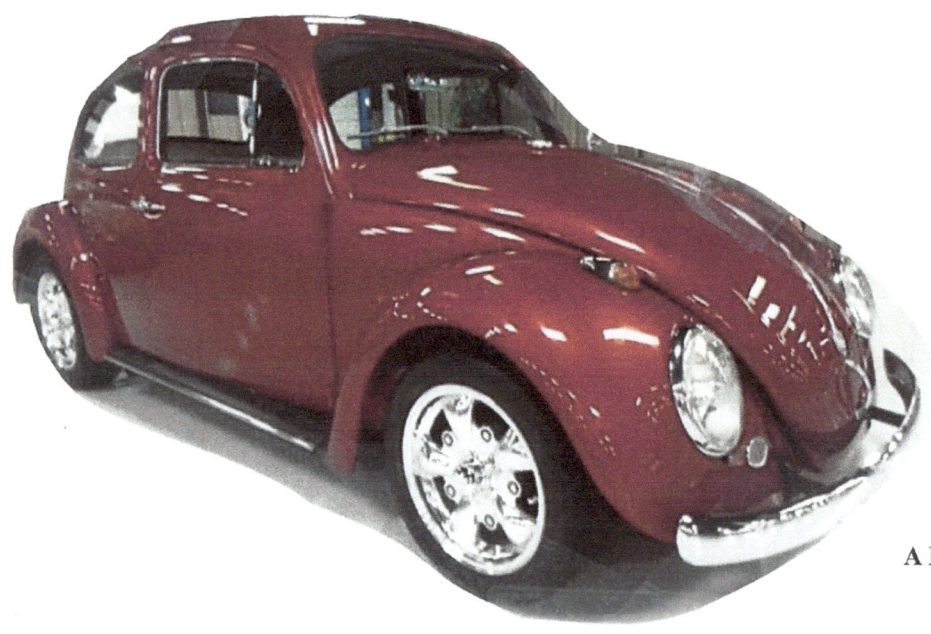

THEY GAVE ME A NEW RED VW BUG
SO, I COULD DRIVE TO HIGH SCHOOL
MY FRIENDS THAT WAS VERY COOL
THE GIRLS KEPT ASKING FOR A RIDE
I COULD ONLY FIT THREE
GAS WAS ONLY $.19 A GALLON

WHY DO MOMS AND DADS
LOVE TO GIVE SURPRISES
UNTIL I AM ONE, I'LL NEVER KNOW
THEIR GIFTS TO ME LEFT ME IN AWE
STARTING WITH A NEW HIGH-TECH CAMERA
NO MORE FILM OR LABS
COUPLED WITH A PERSONAL COMPUTER

AT GRADUATION DINNER THEY SMILED WITH GLEE
HERE LANCE A THIN ENVELOPE WAS PASSED TO ME
IT HAD THE HARVARD LOGO PRETTY AS CAN BE
A SIMPLE LETTER SAID IT ALL
YOUR TUITION PAID IN FULL SEE YOU IN THE FALL
MOM AND DAD SMILED, THERE IS MORE TO COME

YOUR GRANDFATHER LEFT YOU A TRUST
UNLIKE AGE LIMITS IT WAS UP TO US
ITS YOURS IN THIS BANK WITH PLASTIC TO USE
TO MANNEY ZEROS AFTER THE BIG NUMBERS
YOU WILL BE FREE THE WORLD TO SEE

LANCE

HARVARD YEARS

WE HAD TO FLY LEFT THE BUG AT HOME
THE DRESS CODE WAS STRICT
A FEW DAYS EARLY MOM AND I WENT SHOPPING
I WAS NOW 6'-1" TALL 165 LBS IN MY B/D SUIT
WITH HER TASTE EVERYTHING WE SELECTED
IT WAS A TRANSFORMATION EXPERIENCE

I SETTLED IN THE DORM WITH ONE NEW MATE
HE WAS FROM BOSTON, AS MOM KISSED ME GOODBYE
I WOULD FIND AN APARTMENT PERHAPS NEXT YEAR
I DID NOTICE MOM HAD TEARS AS SHE LEFT
SCHEDULE TO CHECK ASSIGNED I WOULD BE
THE COLLEGES WERE EVERYTHING
FROM HEAVEN TO HELL

I NEW I HAD TO BE A FROG IN A POND
THE BASICS TO RELEARN BEFORE
I WAS ALLOWED A COLLEGE CHOICE TO BE
I ALWAYS NEW THIS WAS A MATING GROUND
YOUNG LADIES ABOUND LOOKING FOR A MATE
STILL HAD MY BLOND HAIR EYES OF GREEN
I DID NOT MIND THE LOOKS THEY GAVE ME

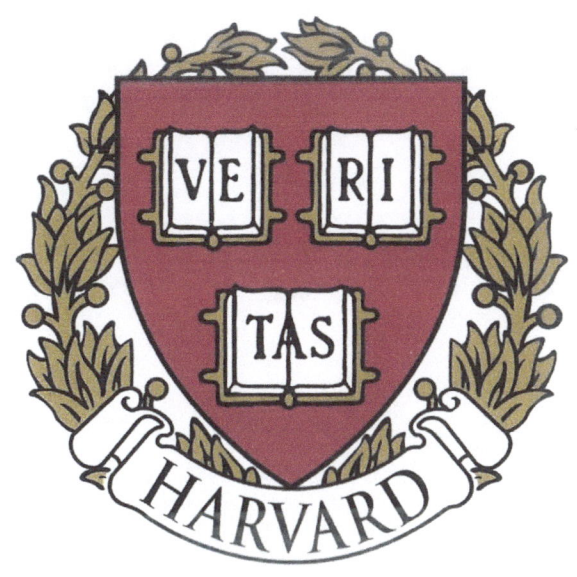

AT THE END OF MY FRESH YEAR
MY PROF SAID TO ME GRADES ARE OUTSTANDING
WE HAVE SPECIAL PROGRAMS AND GROUPS TO JOIN
ALL I WANT TO ENTER AS MANY COLLEGES
SO, I CAN LEARN THE WAYS OF OUR WORLD
WHAT A NOBLE THOUGHT HE SAID TO ME

WENT TO BOSTON WITH MY SURLY MATE
FOR THE SUMMER MONTHS
HE TOLD ME THE SAILING WOULD BE FREE
MOM AND DAD WOULD BE JOINING ME
FOR A FEW WEEKS AT MIDSUMMER NIGHT
GOSH I KNEW THIS WORLD WAS ME

IT WAS OVER IN A FLASH
BACK TO THE DORM IN EVENING TWILIGHT
MY PROF LEFT A NOTE COME SEE ME
TIME AS COME TO PICK A COLLEGE
I HAVE LOVED PHOTOGRAPY FOR MANY A YEAR
I WANT TO SEE THE CREATIVE WORLD THIS YEAR
ART AND SCIENCES IS YOUR FORTAY
ENROLL SEE YOU MID-TERM

I EXPERIENCE MANY MORE COLLEGES
BY THE GRACE OF ELECTIVES
THIS I DID FOR THE NEXT FEW YEARS
POLITICAL SCIENCE AND RELIGION
I FIGURED HAD MADE OUR CURRENT WORLD
I WAS THIRSTY FOR THIS KNOWLEDGE

A YOUNG AVANT-GUARD PROFESSOR
HIS CLASSES WERE STACKED
I BEGGED FOR A SEAT WHICH HE GAVE ME
HIS FIRST WORDS I'LL NEVER FORGET
"AT THE END OF THE SEMISTER
I WILL HAVE GIVEN YOU A NEW WORLD"

THIS STRUCT A CHORD IN ME
LET'S START WITH THE BLUE PLANET
WE NAMED IT EARTH FLOATING IN
UNIVERSE NO WAS MENT TO EXPLAIN
I BRING US TO EARTH VERY FAST
WE ALL KNOW GEOGRAPHY
LET IT GO FORGET IN THE PAST

HIS LECTURES WERE THREE A WEEK
NO EMPTY SEATS IN THE HOUSE
FIRST TO BAT HE SPOKE LOUD AND CLEAR
THINK OF OUR WORLD AS A VERY
LARGE UNIVERSITY
WITH COLLEGES NUMEROUS WHICH
WE WILL CALL COUNTRYS

THE PATTERN YOU SEE ARE ALL THE SAME
LARGE OR SMALL WITH BOARDER LIMITS
MENT TO DEFINE THE CULTURES
OWNERSHIP OF THE OCEANS
WITH A 12 MILE LIMIT THE REST IS FREE

HUMANS IN THESE COUNTRYS ALL THE SAME
ONLY RACE, CULTURE, RELIGION AND POLIOTICS
AND DEFINED BORDERS AND BORDOM
THROUGH EVULOTION AND THEY
WILL KNOW EVERY LASTING CHANGE
HUMAN ANOTOMY I WILL DEFINE

THERE IS ONLY ONE COLOR
THAT RUNS THROUGH US ALL
MOST CREATURES OF THE EARTH
AND MANY OF THE SEA
EXPOSED TO AIR THE COLOR
IS RED

KNEELING WITH BOTH HANDS ON THE GROUND
THE UNIVERSAL BODY WE OWN
RELATES TO MOST ALL CREATURES
HIGH ON THE END LARGE WASTE IS ELIMINATED
LOWER BELOW THE WATER WILL FLOW
THE FOOD WE EAT PROVIDES THE DAILY
ENERGY AND GROWTH OF BODY AND MIND

THE EARLY DOMESTICATION BY PARENTS
MEAN WELL FOR THE CAN ONLY
GIVE YOU WHAT THEIR PARENTS
TOLD THEM SO WELL
THE LINE OF DOMESTICATION ALWAYS
WILL PROVAIL TAKE THE GOOD ONLY
FORGET THE BLACK MAGIC OF THE PAST
YOU LIVE IN THE PRESENT.
YOU CAN MAKE HEAVAN OR HELL LAST
BE FREE TO ENJOY YOUR LIFE

RELEGION BASE IS POLITICS
CONTROL OVER THE MASSES
MONEY ALWAYS THE GOAL
AND A FEW WILL RAISE TO POWER
ALL COUNTRYS HAVE THIS FORM
THE BORDOM IS CREATED
STARTING WARS AND NEIGHBORS DECIMATED
GREED OF POWER MONGERS
THAT WE PLACED IN HIGH ESTIME
HISTORY HAS PROVEN THIS FACT IS TRUE

TIME IN CLASS WITH MORE CONCEPTS TO FOLLOW
MIDTERMS CAME AND NO EXAMS WERE GIVEN
END OF THE SEMESTER AND THAT WAS IT
THE PROF STATED IN A CITY PARK
ALL OF HIS STUDENTS WERE INVITED
FOR HOT DOGS AND BEER, HE WILL FURNISH
BRING YOUR OWN OTHER IF YOU SO CHOOSE
STARTS AT TWO PM AND GRADES READ AT THREE
AT THE END OF APRIL WITH WEATHER DELIGHT
HE STOOD ON THE PICNIC TABLE
SMILING HE SAID YOU ALL GET AN "A"
AND LET THE UNIVERSE GUIDE YOUR FLIGHT

LANCE KNEW HE WOULD GRADUATE IN MAY
WITH LOTS OF PAPER TO HANG ON THE WALL
ONLY THEN DID THEN HE REALIZED
HE HAD NO WALL
HARVARD WAS GREAT AND MANY LADIES
LIKES HE FOUND THE NUMBER WAS FOUR
THEY PARTED WAYS FOR HE KNEW
HE WANTED ONLY THE GREAT UNIVERSITY
TO TAKE AND FIND IMAGES AND EXPLORE

MOM AND DAD WERE ESTADIC WITH PRIDE
WITH HIM IN THE TRADIONAL CAP AND GOWN
AT DINNER HE ASKED THEM TO STORE
THE THINGS HE HAD NO USE FOR
AND HANG HIS PAPER ON THEIR WALL
WHERE ARE YOU GOING? I DON'T KNOW?
I CALL YOU FROM THERE WHE I GET THERE

HE LEARED TO TRAVEL LITE
CARRY ON OR BACK PACK
WITH ALL OF THE THINGS HE NEEDED
TWO HIGH TECK CAMERAS ONLY
WITH STATE OF THE ART LAP TOP
WITH THIS IMAGES AND VIDEOS
THE GREAT UNIVERSITY TO RECORD

HE SUBMITTED FROZEN TIME IMAGES
THAT HE HAD TAKEN THROUGH THE YEARS BEFORE
TO TOP MAGAZINES PHOTO GALLERIES
NEWSPAPERS AND MORETHEY WANTED TO HIRE HIM
AND PUT HIM ON STAFFNE KINDLY SAID NO

OF ALL THE GREAT PLACES TO GO
HE WANTED TO START IN ENGLAND
AND SHOOT LONDON IN THE SNOW
THE OCEAN FLIGHT WAS FAST
HEATHROW CUSTOMS LET HIM GO
AN ODD SHAPHED TAXI DRIVER TO MATCH
FAIRYED HIM TO LONDON IN THE SNOW

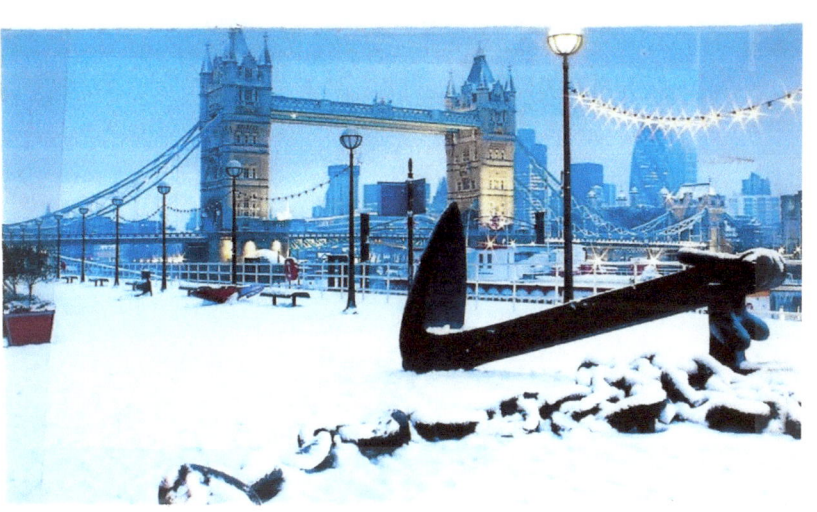

I WALK AROUND AFTER BREAKFAST
I NEED A PAIR OF BOOTS DESIGNED FOR SNOW
THE HOTEL WAS VERY CONTINENTAL
AT TEA TIME HE SAW A FEW
PROFESSIONAL PHOTOGRAPHERS
HE HAD SPOTTED THEM
AND LAUGHED AT THEIR BODY WEAR

STRUNG LIKE BANDELEERS
HUNG DOWN FROM A MILITARY VEST
CAMERAS, LENS SO MANY I LOST COUNT
I AM SURE THEY MADE LOTS OF MONEY
I HAVE NEVER OR EVER CHARGED A FEE
I DID NOT WISH TO MEET THEM
THEY WERE DIFFERENT FROM ME

IN A FEW DAYS I HAD A LAP TOP
FULL OF SNOW FILLED IMAGES
I NOTICED A SIGN IN THE HOTEL LOBBY
COME TO GALA FUND RAISER
TO HELP THE POOR AND NEEDY
TIME DATE AND PLACE
THOUGHT IT WOULD BE FUN
AND CONTRIBUTE A BIT OF POUNDS
SO, I WENT

I LEFT MY SNOW BOOTS IN MY ROOM
STARTED TO DRESS IN LONDONS BEST
A TAXI WITH LARGE DOORS
JUST AS BEFORE WITH HEAD ROOM
I WAS TOLD FOR VERY HIGH HATS
ARRIVING A THE PLACE
A PALACE FOR SURE
MAYBE A VIST BY THE QUEEN

GREATED AT DOOR THEY
PLACED MY WINTER COAT AND HAT
PRETTY LADIES SET BEHIND WHITE TABLES
AN ARRAY OF CREDIT MACHINES
IN LINE LIKE SOLDIERS
STOPPING AT ONE I INSERTED
MY PLASTIC FILLED OUT FORM
STATED THE AMOUNT
THE LADY READ THIS AND
SHOUTED WITH GLEE

I RAN TO THE BAR HOPING TO GET LOST
FOR MY NAME WAS ANOUYMOUS
THE CHAMPAGN WAS GREAT
THROULY ENJOYED THE MEAL
DANCING THEN STARTED
I THOUGHT THEY HAD ASKED
THE LONDON SYNPHONY

I DID NOT HAVE TO LOOK
SHE HAD FOUND ME
TO THE FLOOR WE DANCED
HOLDING HER LIGHTLY AND DESCREET
SHE SAID I HAVE SEEN YOU BEFORE
LET'S FIND A TABLE AND HAVE A CHAT

THE WAITER BROUGHT 2 CLASSES
AND A BOTTLE OF YOU KNOW WHAT
I LOOKED HER AND FOR THE FIRST TIME
MY HEART TO A SPIN LIKE FLIPPIN A DIME
SHE WAS SO BEAUTIFUL HOPED INSIDE AND OUT
HER HAIR WAS RED AND GREEN EYES PURE
MILK WHITE SKIN FOR WHAT I COULD SEE
A GRACEFUL BODY TRIMMED IN HEAVEN

SHE STARTED TO TALK IN A SWEET VOICE
MY NAME IS LAURA O'NEAL TELL ME YOURS
I STUDERED KEEP CALM I SAID TO MYSELF
LANCE E. SCOTT NAMESAKE LANCELOT
WOW SHE SMILED A NIGHT OF THE ROUND TABLE
ONLY OUR SQUARE KITCHEN TABLE

26

I AM A HARVARD GRAD AND I KNOW YOU ARE TOO.
WE BOTH GOT A'S IN THE YOUNG PROFS CLASS
WE WERE IN A SEA OF STUDENTS
YOU HAD NO ROVING EYE NEATHER DID I
IT WAS ALL WE COULD DO TO LISTEN
THE UNFOLDING OF THE GREAT UNIVERSITY
THIS CHANGED MY LIFE AND I SEE IT DID YOU
I HAVE BEEN GIVEN A TRUST THAT
HAS SET ME FREE I BET YOU HAVE ONE TOO
MY GIFT IS TO WRITE BOOKS FOR
WHATS NOW IS HAPPENING IN OUR WORLD

I HAVE SEEN YOUR IMAGES SO MANY
PLACES BEFORE LEFT THE USA
I NOW MET THE AUTHOR
PHOTOGRAPHY IS YOUR GIFT
LET'S TALK AGAIN TOMARROW
I AM STAYING AT THE SAME HOTEL
I 'VE SEEN YOU THERE
LET'S SHARE A WILD TAXI TO GET US THERE

WE MET FOR LUNCH SNOW BOOTS ON
I NOTICED SHE HAD THEM TOO
LUNCH WAS SLOW THE ENGLISH WAY
FISH CHIPS AND GUNINESS
SHE SMILED AND SAID CAN YOU TAKE
MORE OR LESS A FEW DAYS
FOR MORE OF LONDON TO SEE
MAYBE AS MUTUAL COMPANIONS
I KNEW THEN SHE WAS CREATIVE AND STRONG

LANCE, SHE ASKED PLEASE TELL ME
THE BEST ADVISE YOUR MOTHER GAVE TO YOU
WHEN I WAS VERY YOUNG, SHE SCREAMED
"NEVER, NEVER CLIMB A TREE"
IT'S YOUR TURN NOW PLEASE TELL ME
ITS SHORT AND SIMPLE
"DON'T EVER JUMP IN THE BACK SEAT"
THIS ADVISE CAME TO LATE
YOU ARE THE FIRST FRIEND TO KNOW
NOW I CAN TELL YOU WHY

IN MY JUNIOR YEAR IN HIGH SCHOOL
THE FOOTBALL CAPTAIN WAS A RAKE
HE WAS A SENIOR HIS GIRLS SCORES WERE HIGH
SOMEONE SPIKED THE PUNCH AT THE PROM
HE OFFERED ME A RIDE TO COUNT THE STARS
HE DROVE US TO LOVERS LEAP
WITH A KISS OR TWO AND SAID
LET'S JUMP IN THE BACK SEAT

IT WAS OVER IN A TWINKLE WITHOUT THE STAR
HE MADE ME A WOMEN THAT VERY NIGHT
HE NEVER SAID THANK YOU NOR COULD I
ONE MORE CONQUEST TO ADD TO HIS SCORE
THE SUMMER THAT FOLLOWED
I NEW I WAS PREGNANT

MOM WAS COMFORTING DAD DID A BLAST
FOR THE SAKE OF YOUR FUTURE
ONLY ONE THING CAN WE DO
THE GRAPEVINE GAVE US A DOCTOR
THE APPOINTMENT WAS MADE
MOM TOLD ME THE PROCEEDURE
WHEN IT WAS DONE THE SAD EYE
DOCTOR WITH TEARS IN HIS EYES
LOOKED WAY AND DELEIVED THE NEWS
YOU WILL NEVER EVER CONCEIVE A CHILD
IN YOUR WOMB

LANCE KNEW THIS STOREY WAS TRUE
HE ALWAYS PROTECTED PREVIOUS LADYS
HE KNEW WHAT TO DO
LAURA, HE SAID THAT WAS A LONG
TIME AGO YOU HAVE HEALED VERY WELL
TRUST IS GAINED BY TELLING ONLY TRUTH
SOMETIMES IT HURTS, LIES HURT EVEN MORE
SEEMS LIKE WE HAVE BONDED
AND I LIKE YOU FOR SHARING
A CHAPTER IN YOUR LIFE

"STAR DOG"
SPIRITS IN THE
UNIVERSE

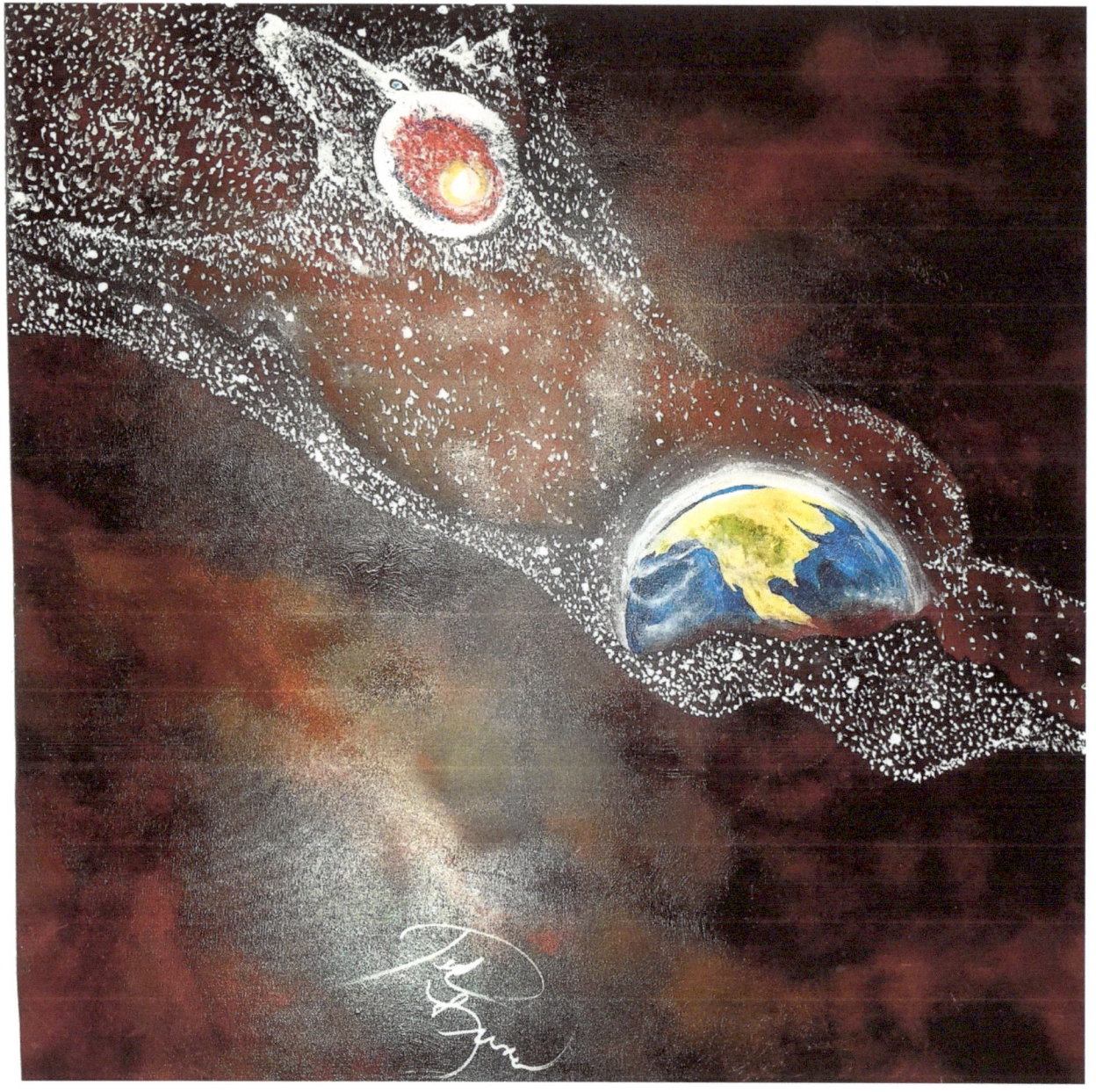

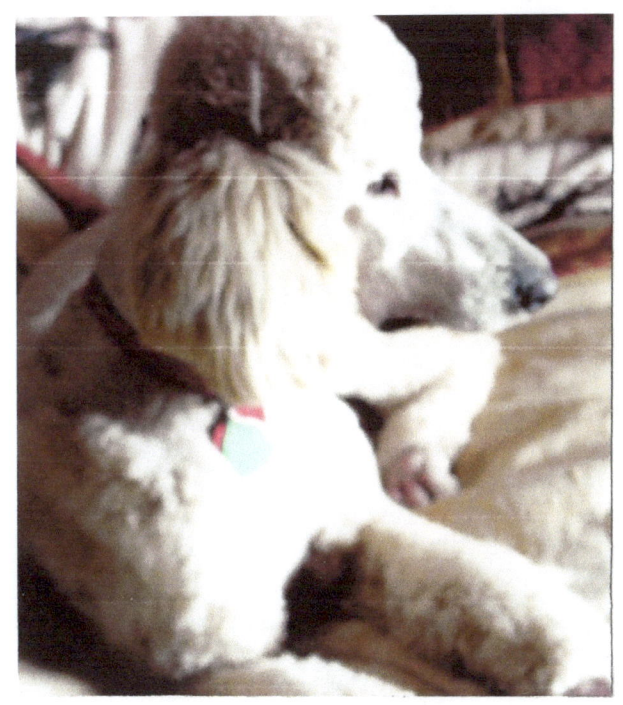

SINISTER SOLSTICE

SIX HOURS BEFORE YOU CAME
I LOST THE LOVE OF MY LIFE
I CRIED A THOUSAND TEARS
TEN HOURS AFTER YOU LEFT
I LOST ANOTHER LOVE OF MY LIFE
I SHED A THOUSAND TEARS MORE

SILENT SUFFERING
NO WORDS TO SPEAK
ACTIONS AND TESTS
DETERMINE THE WORST
OPTIONS DO NOT EXIST
ONLY ONE
GENTAL KINDNESS
THAT ENDS IT ALL

" YOU ARE STAR DOGS NOW"

LOVE, COMPASSION AND UNDERSTANDING
SOMETIMES ARE THE TOOLS OF LIFE'S HURT
RESOLUTION AND KINDNESS
ARE THE ONLY PILLS TO AWAKE
RESOLUTION CLEARS THE SOUL
KINDNESS CLEANSE THE SPIRIT

FOREVER MY SWEETHEARTS
THANKS FOR THE JOY IN MY LFE
TIFFANY 2 AND FOXY
IT WAS TIME TO GO

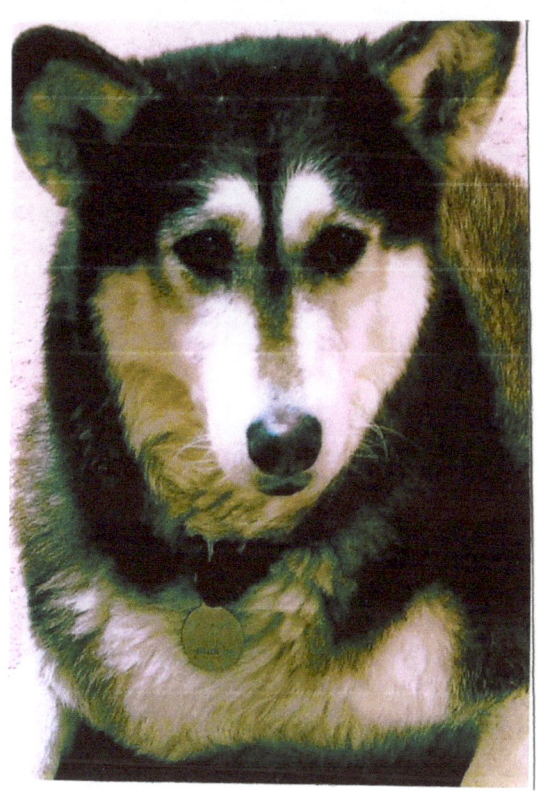

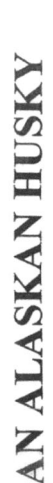

AN ALASKAN HUSKY

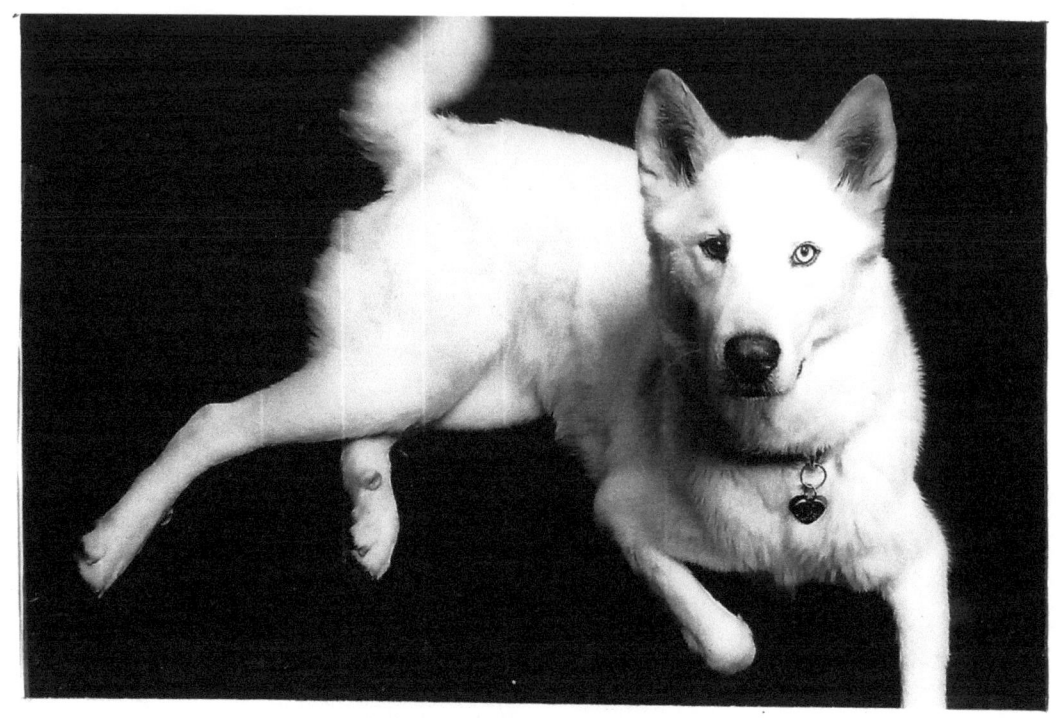

DESTING "DES"

THE BERNALILLO COUNTY ANIMAL SERVICES PICKED LEILA UP ON JUNE 15, 2018.
I HAD BEEN IN MOURNING FOR 30 DAYS WITH MY LOSS OF TIFFANY TWO.
THANKS FOR QUICK ACTION BY REGINA AND STEPHANIE FROM A PHONE CALL FROM
THE SHELTER BY A CONTACT THAT REGINA KNEW BECAUSE HER PREVIOUS WORK
IN ANIMAL RESCUE THEY GAVE LEILA TO HER. LOVE AT FIRST SIGHT BY ALL PRESENT.
WHEN THEY BROUGHT HER TO ME IT WAS LOVE AT FIRST SIGHT. AND WILL REMAIN
THAT WAY FOREVER. THE SHELTER HAD NO INFORMATION ON THE PREVIOUS OWNER.
REGINA SUGGESTED WE RENAME HER DESTING NOW YOU KNOW HER NAME SAKE.
I NURSED HER THROUGH PUPPY HOOD AT A MODEST COST OF 3 TV REMOTES, 2 PAIR OF
GLASSES, A COUPLE OF PAIR OF OLD SHOES, DIDN'T LIKE ANWAY. SHE WENT FROM 60
POUNDS AND THE RUNS TO A HEALTHY 84 POUNDS IN A SHORT TIME. BUT BEST OF ALL
HER LOVE, KINDNESS, INTELLIGENCE, UNDERSTANDING OF WORD VOICE COMMANDS
AND COMPANION SHIP IS BETTER THAN MY PREVIOUS WIFES OR LADY FRIENDS.
THERE ARE NO STRANGERS BECAUSE SHE IS LOVING AND GENTLE TO ALL.
I KNOW DESTING IS MY DESTING.

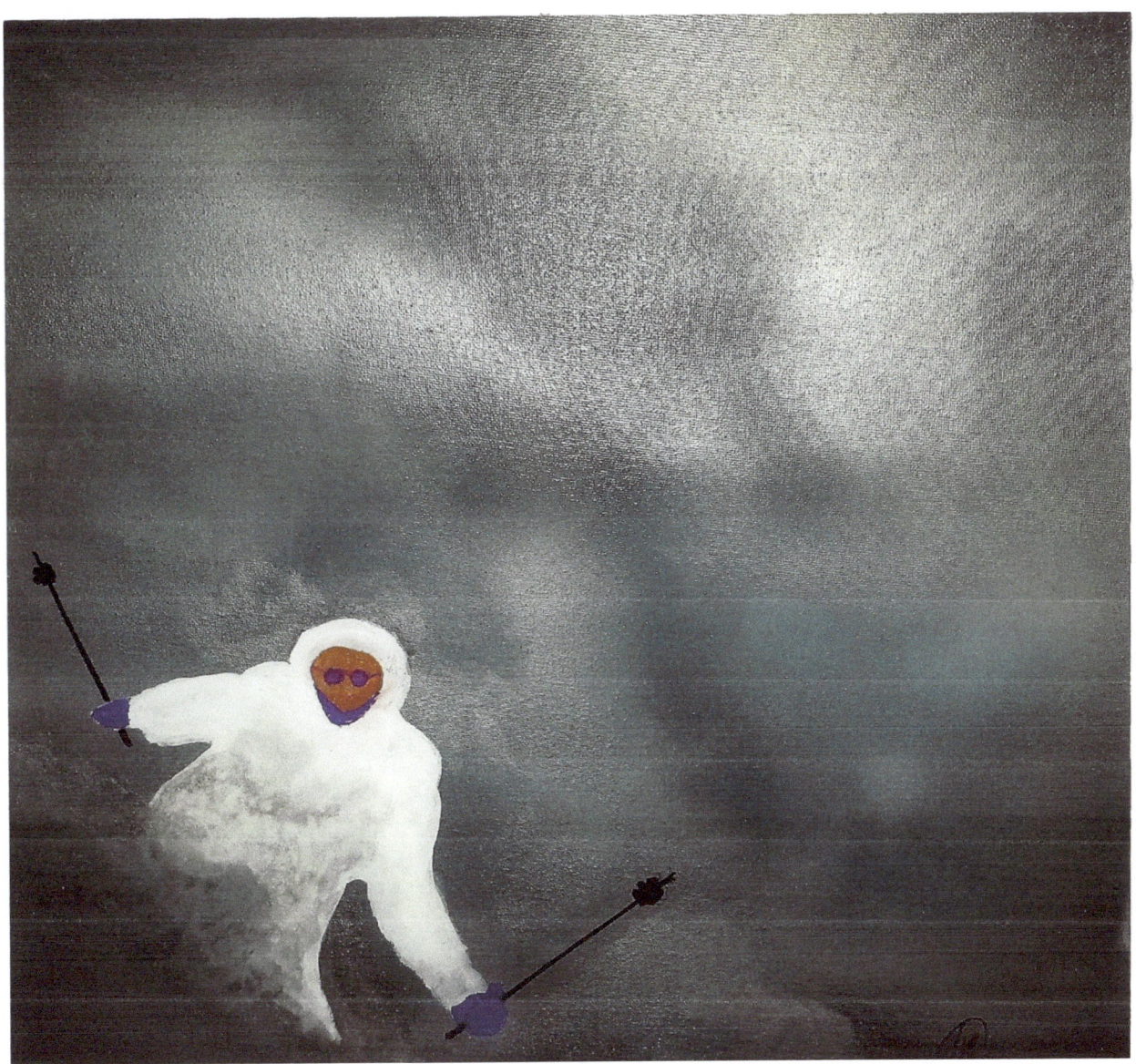

SKING ON ICE

DOWN THE FALL
LINE I GO
STRIAGHT AND TURNS
HIGH PITCHED
EERIE SOUNDS
ONLY I CAN HEAR
THE SKIS SING
AS THEY CUT
THE HARD FROZEN
ICE WITH A DUSTIN
OF NEW FALLEN
SNOW
SOME DAY THE SUN
WILL SHINE AND
TAKE THE ICE AWAY
BUT IT WON'T
HAPPEN FOR ME
TODAY
FELL ONLY ONCE
ON THIS GLIDE DOWN
THE HILL
TUMBELD WITH MY
MOUTH FULL OF
SNOW
THIS COLD WINTER
DAY SMUG AT THE
LODGE I WOULD NOT
STAY TILL I HAVE
SKIED ALL THE ICE
ON THIS COLD
WINTERS DAY

CALVIN AND HOBBES
CAMEOS WITH SUSIE DERKINS

HA THA HAY BILL
WATTERSON PERSONA EXTRAORDINAIR
ODE FOR YOU WITH LOVE
FANS NUMBERED IN MILLIONS
YOU GAVE THEM JOY AND DELIGHT
CREATING CALVIN AND HOBBES
WITH SO MANY STORIES THAT YOU TOLD
LET ME CALL HIM CALVIN THE BOLD
YOU AGED HIM AT SIX
HOBBES CAME HANGING FROM A TREE
ONLY TO BE REAL WITH CALVIN TO SEE.

WHERE CAN I START PERHAPS A MENU TO BE
BLANK ARE FOUR SPACES SOMETIMES A PAGE
WAITING IN ANTICIPATION
FOR YOUR TALENTS TO SING
IMAGINATION, PUNCHED WITH HUMOR AND WIT
SOCIAL COMMENTS PREVAIL MIXED WITH REALITY
YOUR OTHER CHARACTORS ARE DELIGHTFUL
OF COURSE ADDING TO CALVINS PLIGHT.

SUSIE DERKENS I SURE WAS CALVINS LOVE
OF COURSE HE NEVER TOOK HER
TO SMOOTCH CITY
HANDLING HER ONLY WITH WORDS OF FRIGHT
BOTTOM LINE SHE WOULD ALWAYS WIN.

ARCHITECTURE

ROMANESQUE RIVIVAL IS LIKE PROSE
GOTHIC IS LIKE POETRY
LIFTING SPIRITS TO THE SKY
JUST ONE EXAMPLE THE ARCH
TO OPEN WALLS
FOR TRAVEL OR WINDOWS

THE HALF CIRCLE ROMAN ARCH
RETURNS YOUR SPIRIT BACK TO EARTH
THE POINTED GOTHIC ARCH
SENDS YOUR SPIRIT TO THE HEAVENS
IN TOTAL CONCEPT GOTHIC
IS AN NATURAL EVALUTION

THIS BEAUTIFUL CHAPEL FOR
ITS POINT IN TIME
IS THE FINEST RESOLVED
STATEMENT OF GOTHIC
BOTH INSIDE AND OUT
THE NUNS MADE IT HAPPEN

THE FRENCH ARCHITECT AND SON
ANTIONE MOULY DIED BEFORE
IT WAS FINISHED HIS SON FINISHED IT
BUILT BY MASONS ANY MANY
CRAFTSMAN FROM FRANCE
THAT WERE STILL WORKING
AT THE CATHERAL WITH
THE SAME MATERIALS

IT SOON BECAME APPARENT
THAT THE CHOIR LOFT AT THE BACK
ABOVE THE MAIN ENTRY
HAD NO PLANNED ACCESS
ARCHITECT'S OMISSION OR ERROR
WE WILL NEVER KNOW

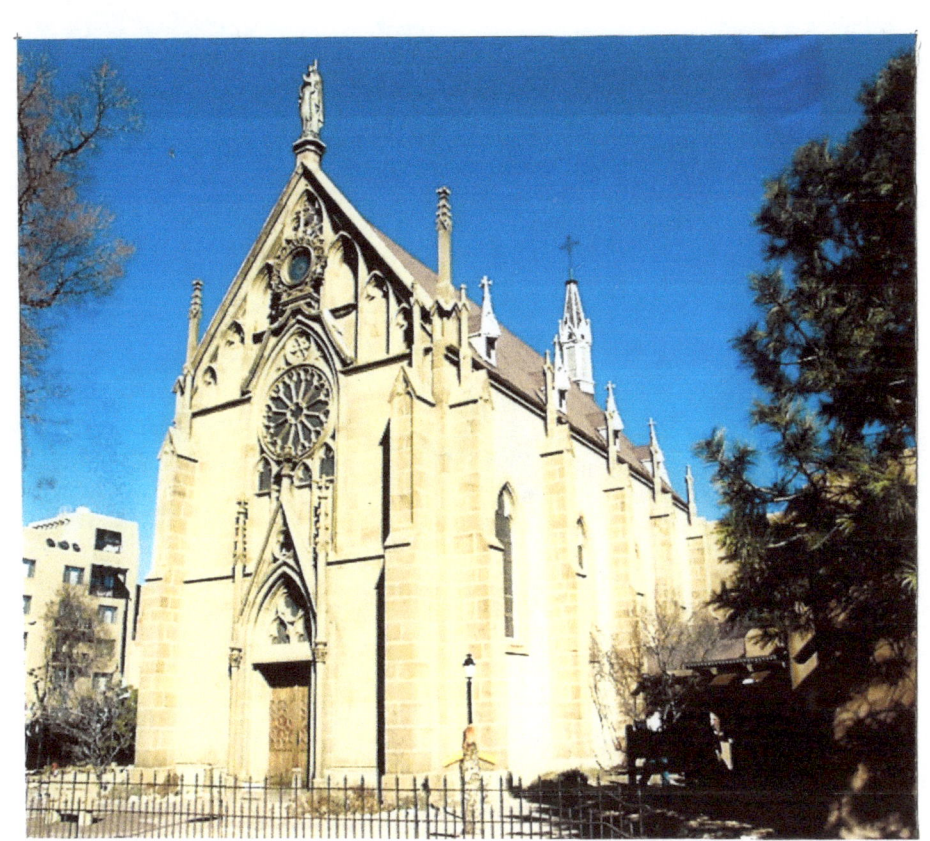

WHERE ANGELS SING
LORRETO CHAPEL SANTA FE

33

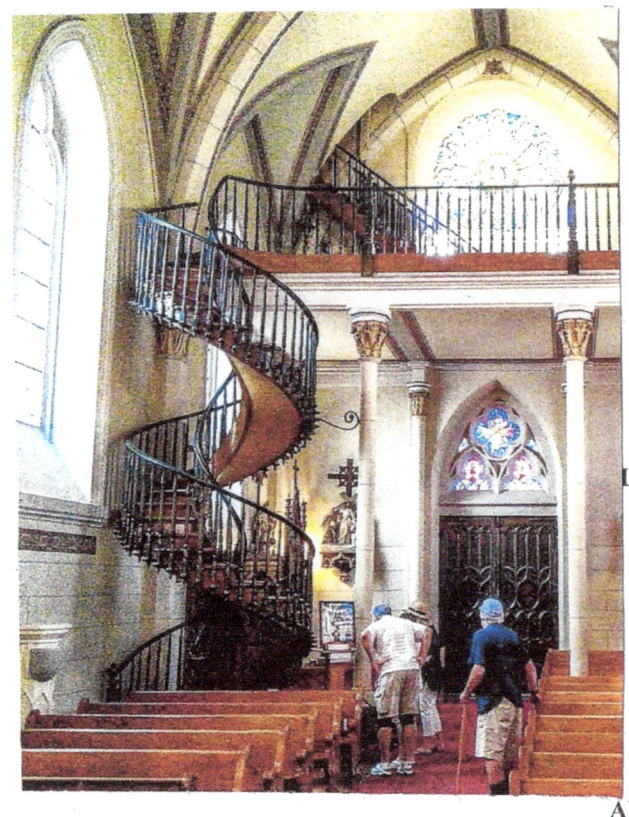

MIRACULOUS STAIR

LEGENDS AND MYSTERYS
PROBABLY SOME ARE TRUE
THE NUNS KNEW WHAT TO DO
THE FRENCH CARPENTER
MAYBE FOR PENANCE

OR LOVE OF HIS WORK
OR MAYBE A REINCARTION
OF ST. JOSEPH ON EARTH
WE WILL NEVER KNOW
HISTORY HAS FOUND HIS NAME
MAYBE ITS NOT TRUE

HOW HE BEGAN IT WAS ONLY
IN HIS MIND NEVER DID THINK
HE WOULD CREATE A WORK
OF ART A WORLD CLASS ICON
IN LEAGUE OF THE MONA LISA
LENARDO WOULD HAVE LOVED HIM

THE NUMBERS THAT FOLLOW
ARE DOCUMENTED FACTS
8" RISERS TIMES 33 EQUAL 22 FEET
NAVE FLOOR TO CHOIR FLOOR
TWO FULL TURNS WITH NO
CENTRAL SUPPORT

FOR MORE FACTS THEY ASKED
URBAN WEIDNER TO EVALUATE
AND DOCUMENT THE CONSTRUCTION
IT WAS GENIOUSLY SIMPLE IT WAS
ALL HELD TOGETHER WITH
WOODEN PEGS

THEY THEN ASKED A WOOD EXPERT
TO FIND THE SPECIES OF THE WOOD
TWO YEARS LATER HE CAME
TO SANTA FE TO STATE HIS FINDINGS
IT WAS A SPECIAL HIGH COUNTRY
SPRUCE THAT GREW ONLY
ABOVE THE ELEVATION OF 10,000 FEET

NO ONE THOUGHT TO LOOK
AT THEIR BACK DOOR
WERE THE SPRUCE FORESTS
AT THIS ELEVATION
THE CARPENTER KNEW
AND MUST HAVE HAD HELP
TO SAW THE LOGS INTO PLANKS

SOAKED IN WATER FILLED TUBS
EASY TO BEND WHEN DRY
THEY WOULD HOLD THEIR SHAPE
EACH TREAD AND RISER
ARE EXACTLY THE SAME
STILL VERY MUCH A MIRACLE

THE CHOIR IN GOWNS
STEPPED THESE STEPS FOR
MANY YEARS
THIS WAS THE START
WHERE ANGELS SING

THE NATURAL ACOUSTICS
OF THE REFLECTION FROM
THE FLOOR, WALLS AND CEILING
ARE THE BEST YOU CAN EVER HEAR
WITH-OUT MODERN APPLIFICATION
SOUNDS AND TONES
THAT ARE HUMANLY CLEAR

EACH YEAR AROUND CHRISTMAS TIME
SANTA FE'S WOMEN ONSOMBLE
PRESENT SONGS OF THE SEASON
ACCAPELA IN PRESSIOUS HARMONY
BRING A TISSUE TO WIPE
THE TEARS OF DELIGHT

TRULY THE PLACE
WHERE ANGELS SING

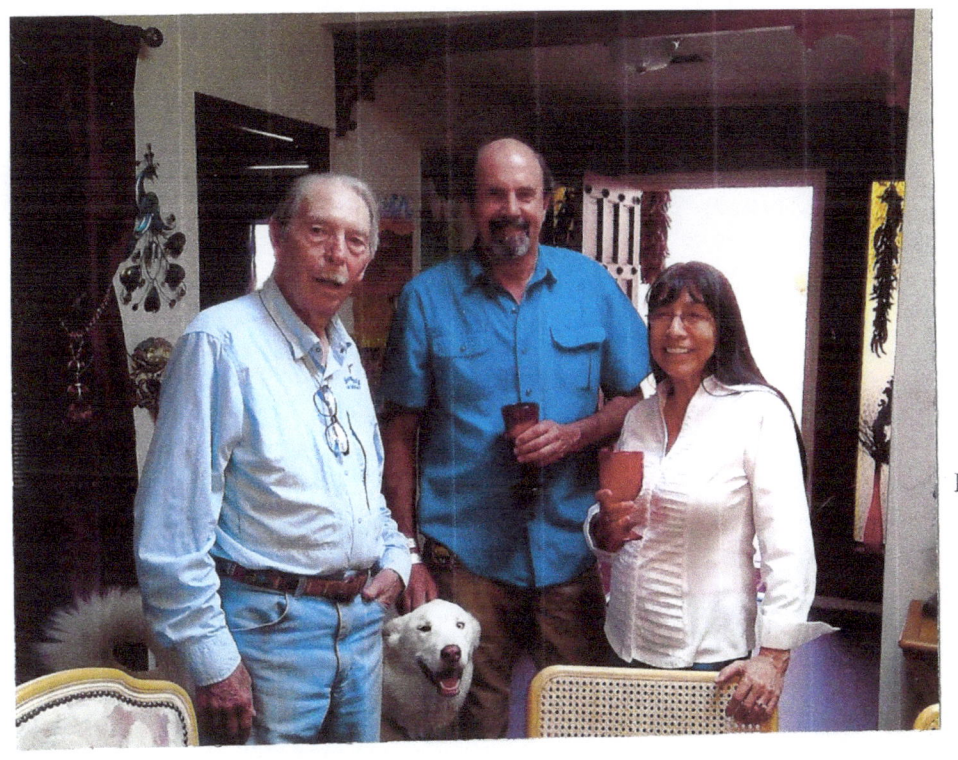

TWO BEAUTIFUL SPIRITS
SEAL THEIR DESTINY

UNDER THE SHADE OF ANCIENT COTTONWOOD TREES
IN A PRISTINE GREEN GRASS SURROUND BY FLOWERS
SET 300 WHITE CHAIRS
THE SKY WAS GREY AND THE MUSIC WAS SWEET
THE TATOOED LADY PILOTED A DRONE OVERHEAD
THE DESTINY CEREMONY WAS TO BEGAN
THE BRIDESMAIDS ENTERED FROM THE LEFT
THE GROOMSMENS ENTERED FROM THE RIGHT
THEY STOOD TOGATHER IN FRONT OF THE CLERIC

THE TIME WAS SET PRECISELY AT 4:00 PM
A HEARTBEAT LATER THE UNIVERSE SENT
IT'S BLESSING, WINDS OF GALE FORCE
SENDING BOUQUETS OF FLOWERS
SMALL BRANCHES OF LEAVES AND TWIGS
MIXED WITH DEW DROPS OF HAPPY TEARS
THE GROOM BELOWED WITH OUT THE MIC
WE WILL RECONVENE AT THE SAGEBRUSH INN

IN TUNE WITH THE UNIVERSE I HAVE SEEN
THIS BLESSING MANY TIMES BEFORE
AT OUTDOOR SERVICES AT THE GRAVE SITES
CELEBRATIONS AND DEDICATIONS
IT STARTS WITH THE WIND WAYWARD IT IS NOT
BALLOONS AND POSTERS FLY TO THE SKY
THE DEW DROPS GROUP AND BECOME RAIN
PEOPLE SCATHER IN MUCH THE SAME WAY

CLERIC VOWS ENHANCED
EACH MADE SPECIAL PROMISES
RINGS EXCHANGED WITH THE
WORDS I NOW PROCOUNCE YOU
THEY EMBRESSED
WAYNE LIFTED PAT
FOR THE MOST WONDERFUL EVER KISS
CHEERS AND CLAPPING DROWNED THE HALL
DINNER AND DANCING
BUT THAT'S NOT ALL
MY MEASURE OF LIFE IS NOT FINANCIAL
THE TRUE VALUE IS SIMPLE
FAMILY AND FRIENDS ARE THE MARK
300 PLUS PAT AND WAYNE ARE MILLIONARES

THEODORO CORONA LUNA
19 AUGUST 2018

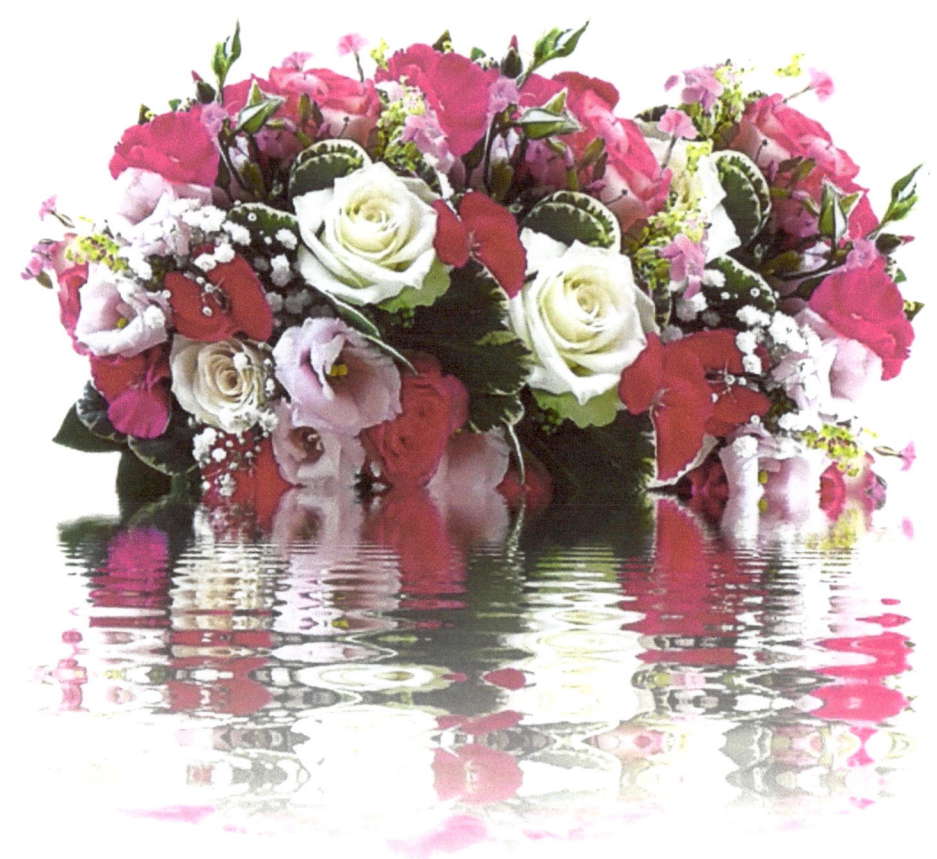

BOUQUET REQUIEM

RESTING IN REPOSE
IN FLORAL SHOPS
AND GROCERY STORES
YOU AND I TAKEN A BUNCH
FOR A TRUE LOVE
SOMETIMES AT HOME

THE GREETING ALWAYS
AWE AND JOY
THE SEARCH FOR THE
GLASS VASE BEGINS
IF IT COULD SPEAK
THE SECRETS IT WOULD NEVER TELL

OFF CAME THE PLASTIC PRISON
SEPERATION WITH AROMA
GENTLE SLANTED CUTS
FOR EACH OF THE STEMS
TO GIVE NEW LIFE
IN A POOL OF SUGARED WATER

ARRANGED IN BEAUTY
RESTING IN A PLACE OF HONOR
CHERISED TILL THEY WILT
AND SOON BEGAN TO DIE
THE BURIAL IN THE TRASH
NO MARKER TO BE GIVEN

LIKE IN LIFE THE STOREY
IS TRUE SEIZE THE DAY
BLOOM LIKE THE FLOWERS
IN SPIRIT DON'T BE SAD
THEN YOU DON'T HAVE TO CRY
AND NEVER SAY GOODBYE

THEODORO CORONA LUNA
APRIL 11, 2019

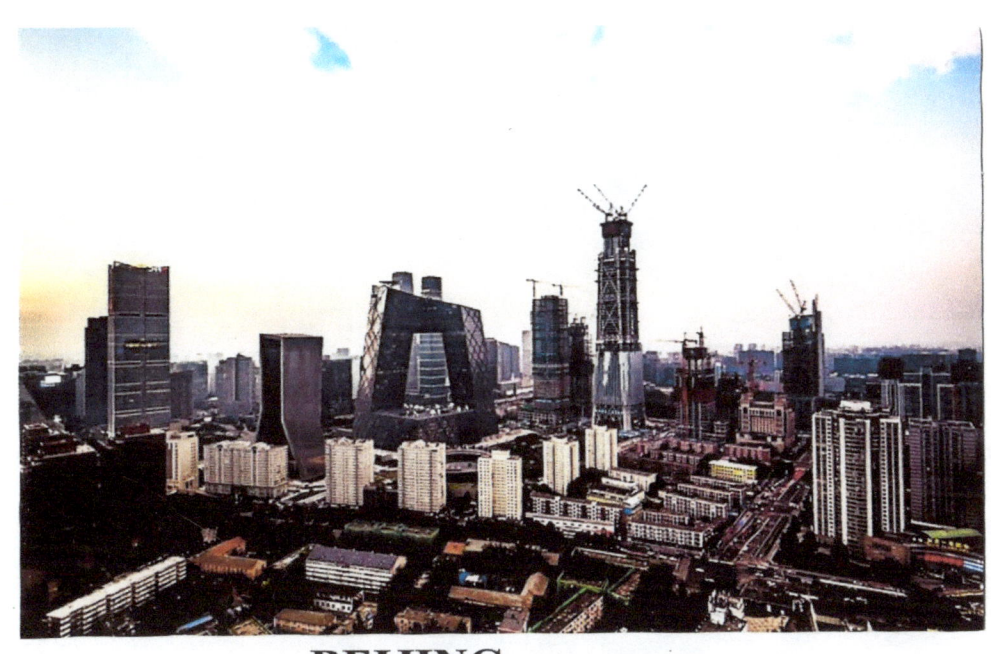

BEIJING ON A CLEAR DAY

SUZANNE AND I PARTED COMPANY A FEW MONTHS AGO, MY TESUQUE HOUSE HAD ONLY TIFFANY AND CHAMPAGNE (POODLES) FOR COMPANY. SHE WAS GREAT COMPANY IN OUR TRAVELS TO MEXICO AND EUROPE. THUS, I WANTED TO GO TO CHINA AND JAPAN. I KNOW THE BEST COST WISE WAY IS TO BOOK A TOUR WITH AAA AND WE SET A DATE. I ALSO KNEW THAT YOU COULD SITE CHANGE ON ANYTHING AS LONG AS YOU HAD AN OPEN-ENDED RETURN FLIGHT. WAITING AT THE INTERNATIONAL AIRPORT IN SAN FRANCISCO SUZANNE TRIED TO REACH ME FOR HER STEP-FATHER HAD DIED. I NEVER RECEIVED THE MESSAGE. THE NON-STOP FLYING HOTEL IN THE SKY WAS WONDERFUL WE LANDED EARLY EVENING IN BEIJING. WE WERE MET AND TAKEN TO A VERY NICE HIGH RISE HOTEL. THEY BOOKED ME ON THE 8TH FLOOR. OUR TOUR GROUP HAD ONLY EIGHT PEOPLE. THE ROOM HAD EVERYTHING AND OUT THE WINDOW I COULD SEE MOST PARTS OF THE CITY. IN THE MORNING THE ROOM HAD A CANISTER FULL OF HOT SOUP, FIRST TIME I LEARNED TO ENJOY SOUP FOR BREAKFAST. IN VIEWING THE STREET BELOW, I SAW WORK MEN DRESSED IN SUITS CARRING A METAL LUNCH BUCKET HEADING TO THE CONSTRUCTION SITE OF A NEW BUILDING. MY CHINA ADVENTURE WAS TO BEGIN AND I WAS FULL OF AWE AND ANTICIPATION. ENTER ONE OF MY TOUR TRAVEL COMPANION GINNY LUKASZEWSKI A PRETTY YOUNG LADY FOR THE CHINA EXPERIENCE, WE BECAME PLATONIC FRIENDS AND SHE WAS FUN TO BE WITH.

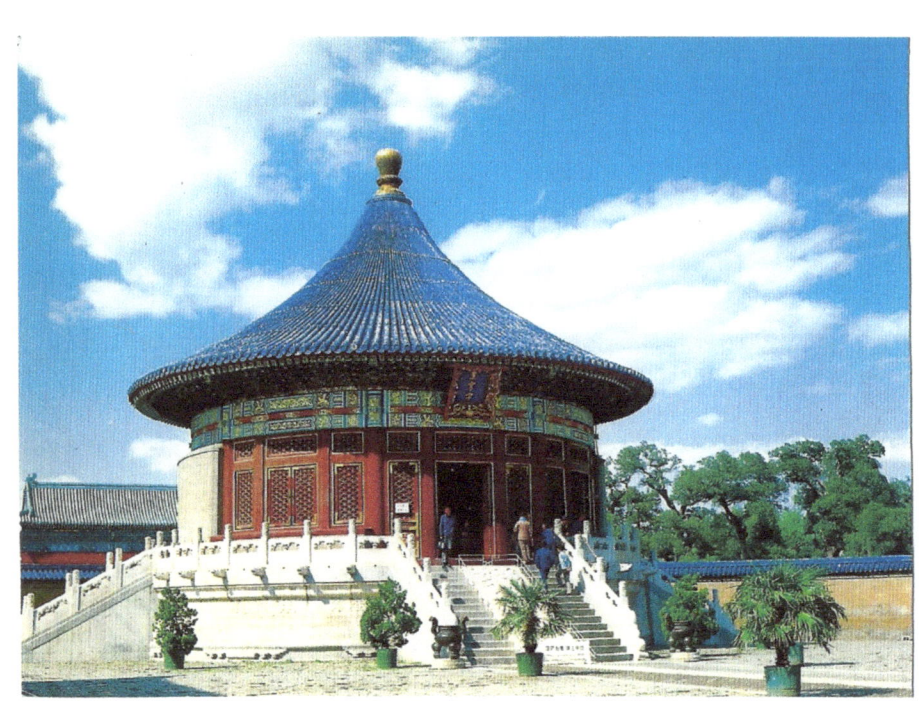

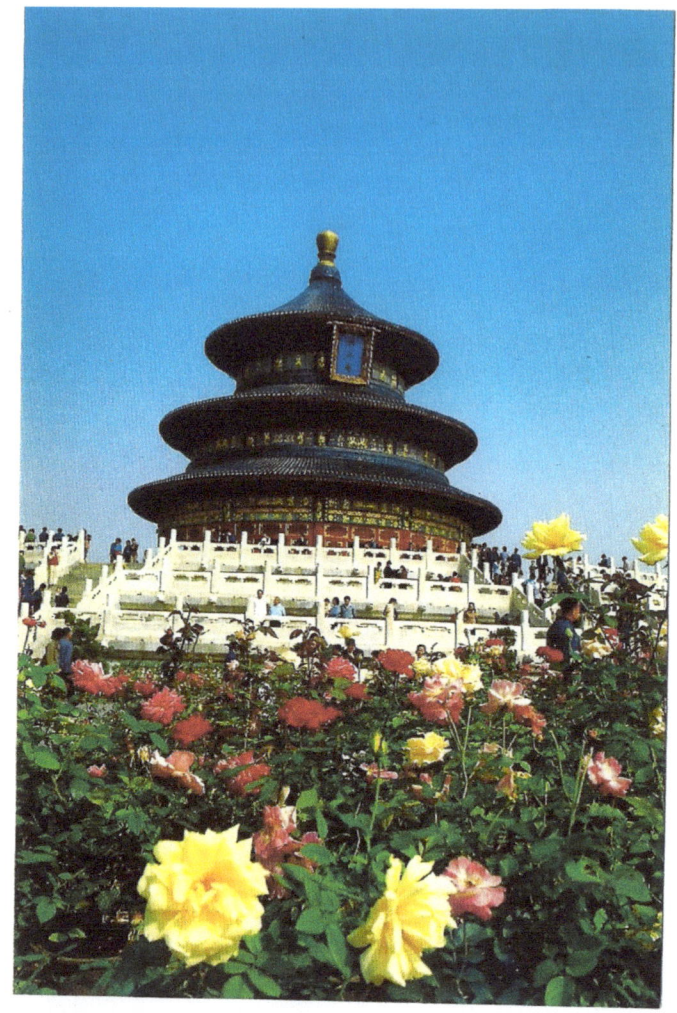

HALL OF IMPERIAL VAULT OF HEAVEN
GINNY AND I CAPTURED SO MANY IMAGES FOR ME
IT COULD MEAN ANOTHER BOOK JUST ON CHINA.
WE SOON DID AND TRAVELED ON OUR OWN.
ONE EXCEPTION WE DID JOIN THE TOUR FOR ONE
NIGHT TO SEE THE BEIJING OPERA. OF COURSE
IT WAS SONG IN CHINESE AND BEAUTIFUL IN COSTUMES
WE BOTH STARTED TO FALL ASLEEP AS THE
LAST ACT ENDED THEN BACK IN THE VAN TO
HOTEL AND PLAN WHAT TO DO TOMARROW.

A FESTIVAL AT TEMPLE OF TIANTAN
ALL OF THE FLOWERS WERE IN FULL BLOOM
AND THE GROUNDS WERE IMPECCABLY GROOMED
NO PHOTOS COULD BE TAKEN IN THE INTERIOR
I RECORDED IT IN MY MEMORY

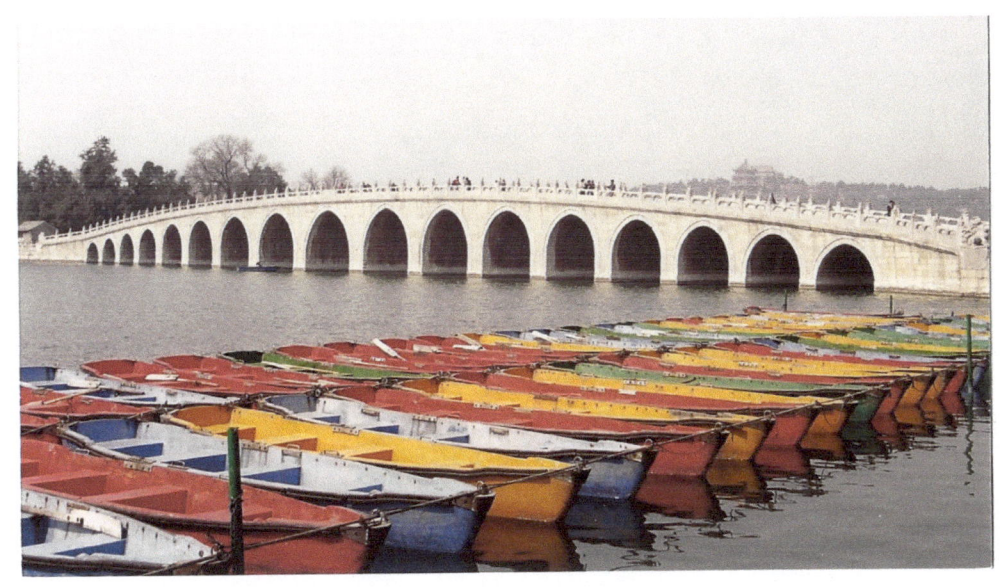

ON THE RIVER
TAKE A CLOSE LOOK AT THE BRIDGE
THE BOATS FOR THE RIVER CRUISE
HAD TO BE SMALL AND NOTE
NO CANAPÉS FOR SUN PROTECTION
AN GREAT DEAL OF TIME OF DAY
WAS UNDER THE SKY OF SMOG
SUN PROTECTIONS WERE HATS

MILL LUMBER DELEVERY
BEIJING STYLE
I REALLY THINK THIS WAS FOR THE
SAKE OF THE TOURISTS
IN THE OLD SECTION MANY OTHER
MEANS OF TRANSPORT OF GOODS
I AM SURE IT WAS FOR THE TOURISTS
THE HUMAN MOTOR OF ANCIENT
TIMES AT LEAST GAVE AN INSIGHT

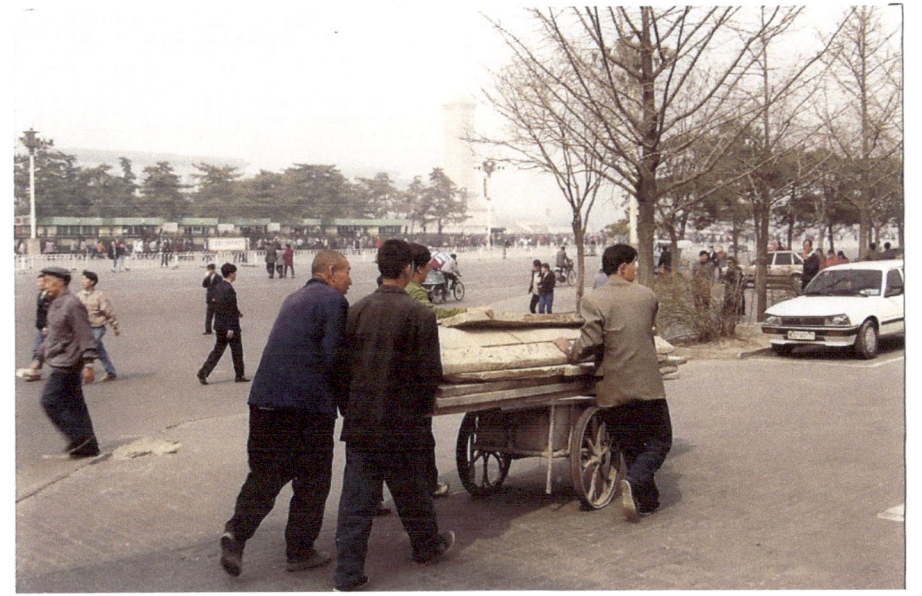

39

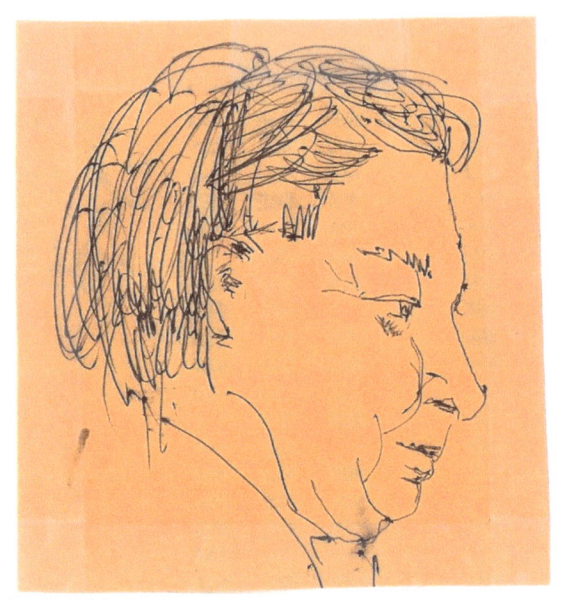
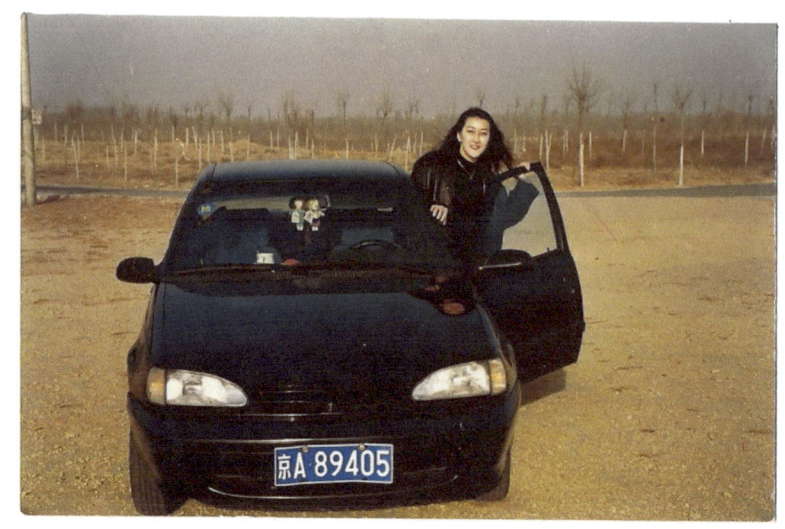

SARAH LEE

ON THE TOP FLOOR OF THE HOTEL THEY HAD A MEDIA ROOM WHICH WAS SMALL AND HAD A SMALL BAR AND KARAOKE SET UP. LATE ONE NIGHT I WENT THERE FOR A NIGHT CAP. THERE ONLY WOMEN ON THE WAIT STAFF BUT A COVEY OF BUSINESS JAPANESE MEN HAVE DRINKS AND SINGING HAVING A BALL. I ORDERED A CHIVAS AND RELAXED AND NOTICED ONE PRETTY LADY LOOKING AT ME. FINISHED MY DRINK LEFT AND WENT
BACK TO MY ROOM. NEXT NIGHT I WENT BACK, SAME JAPANESE MEN THERE DOING WHAT THEY DID THE NIGHT BEFORE. AFTER MY SECOND CHIVAS ONE OF THE MEN CAME TO ME AND PERFECT ENGLISH ASKED IF I WOULD JOIN HIM IN A KARAOKE DUET. HE HAD A WONDERFUL VOICE AND MINE MATCHED HIS. AFTER MANY SONGS THE GROUP WOULD NOT LET US SIT DOWN. WHEN WE DID THE PRETTY LADY CAME OVER AND FILLED MY GLASS WITH CHIVAS AND SET DOWN BESIDE ME., SHE WAS THE MANAGER OF THE MEDIA ROOM AND TOOK A LIKING TO ME. SHE SAID IF I WOULD MEET HER IN THE MORNING, SHE WOULD TAKE ME AROUND BEIJING IN HER CONVERTIBLE.
IS 9:00 OK SHE SMILED AND SAID SEE THEN. SHE TOOK ME PLACES THAT TOURISTS NEVER GO. WE STARTED AT THE BEIJING ZOO. TO ME IT WAS AN ANIMAL PRISON, IRON CAGES WITH CONCRETE FLOORS, ANIMALS BORED AND SLEEPING. SHE DROVE TO A VERY NICE RESTURANT FOR LUNCH. ORDERED PEKING DUCK AND I KNEW THAT PEKING WAS THE ANCIENT NAME OF BEIJING, NOW IT WAS ONLY A DUCK. IN THE DAYS THAT FOLLOW SHE TOOK ME PLACES THAT WERE THE TRUE FABRIC OF BEIJING. THE OLD AREA AND SO MANY OTHER PLACES THAT HAD ME IN AWE. MANY MORE NIGHTS AT THE MEDIA ROOM, CHIVAS WAS ON THE HOUSE, KARAOKE TOO. SHE GAVE ME A SKETCH SHE HAD DONE ON THE PAPER MENU. I LEARNED THAT THE CHINESSE HAD A VERY HIGH MORAL CODE WHEN IT CAME TO BEDDING. THIS WOULD ONLY OCCUR IF YOU WERE MARRIED. NO HOTEL EMPLOYEE WAS ALLOWED IN A GUEST ROOM EXCEPT FOR THE MAIDS. I KNEW THAT SARAH WANTED ME TO TAKE HER TO THE UNITED STATES. SHE ASSUMED I WAS A RICH AMERICAN. SHE GAVE ME A GOOD LUCK CHARM, HANGS IN MY TRUCK TODAY. I GAVE HER MY PURPLE DOWN VEST AND SAID GOODBYE. SHE WROTE ME SEVERAL LETTERS. I NEVER REPLIED.

40

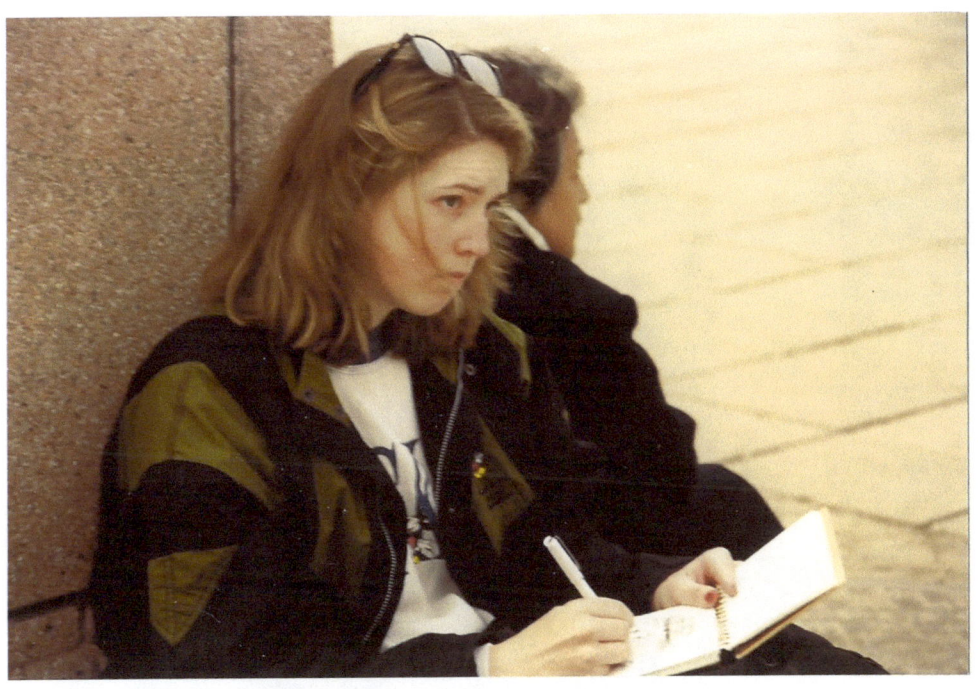

GINNY IN BEIJING
I TOOK THIS WHILE SHE WAS PENSIVE
AND RECORDING HER FOCUSED
THOUGHTS IN HER DIARY

BACK IN THE STATES SHE WROTE
ME SEVERAL LETTERS THE LAST
INCLUDED HER FIRST POEM AND
EXPLAINED THAT IS WAS ABOUT
TROUBLED FRIEND AND TO ME
IT WAS A VERY SAD WAY OF LIFE.
I INCLUDED THIS FOR A
DIFFERENT POINT OF VIEW
SHE DIDN'T NAME IT

HE TREASURES HIS MISERY
A PERFECT WRETCH
HIS AGONIES ARE AN
ORGASMIC JOY

BITTER PILLS OF HIS OWN
MAKING, HE SWALLOW'S THEM
DUTIFULLY A HELL CRAFTED
WITH CARE

HE EAGERLY INHIBITS THE DEPTHS
WHAT KIND OF MAN IS THIS?
EVERY TWIST OF THE KNIFE
IN HIS OWN HAND

YET, SPY THE SATISFIED GLEAM
IN HIS EYE HE HAS FOUND
NO HAPPINESS AND YET
TORMENTING DEMON

BELOVED CHILD OF SACRIFICE
HOW PURILE HOW SELFISH
TO CAST HIMSELF IN A TRAGIC ROLE
HE PLAYS THE PART WITH RELISH

HE REVELS IN CATASTROPHE
SO STOIC AND STRONG
THE ONLY REAL TRAGESTY
HIS SINCERE BELIEF IN IT ALL

/S/ GINNY LUKASZEWSKI

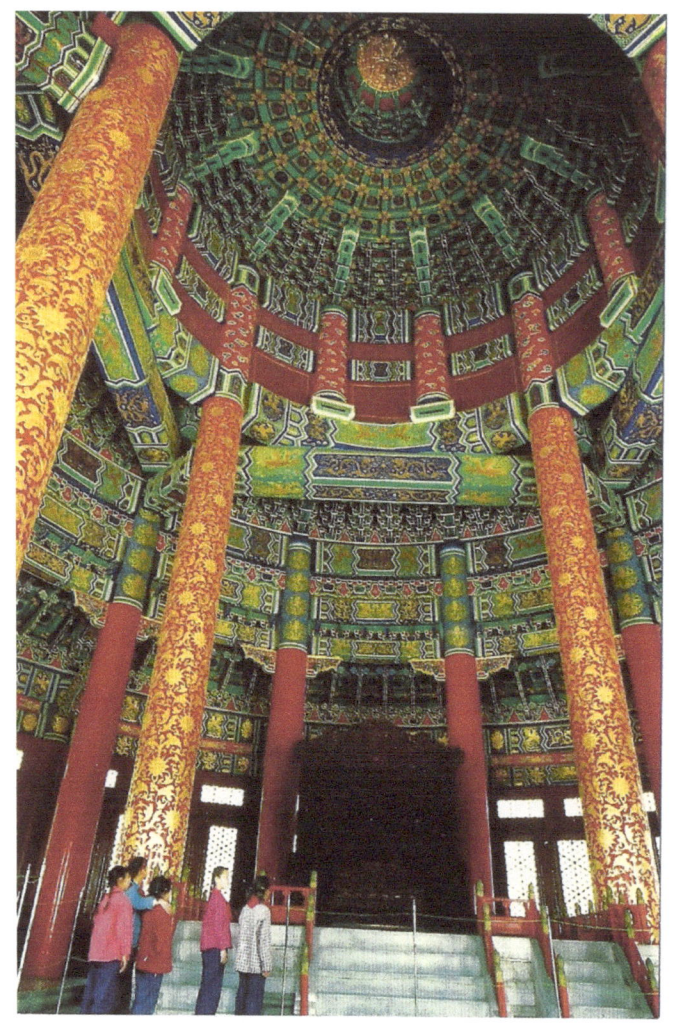

THE GREAT PILLAR
MAGNICENT ARTICULATED
ANCIENT ARCHITECTURE
IN IT'S OWN GLORY

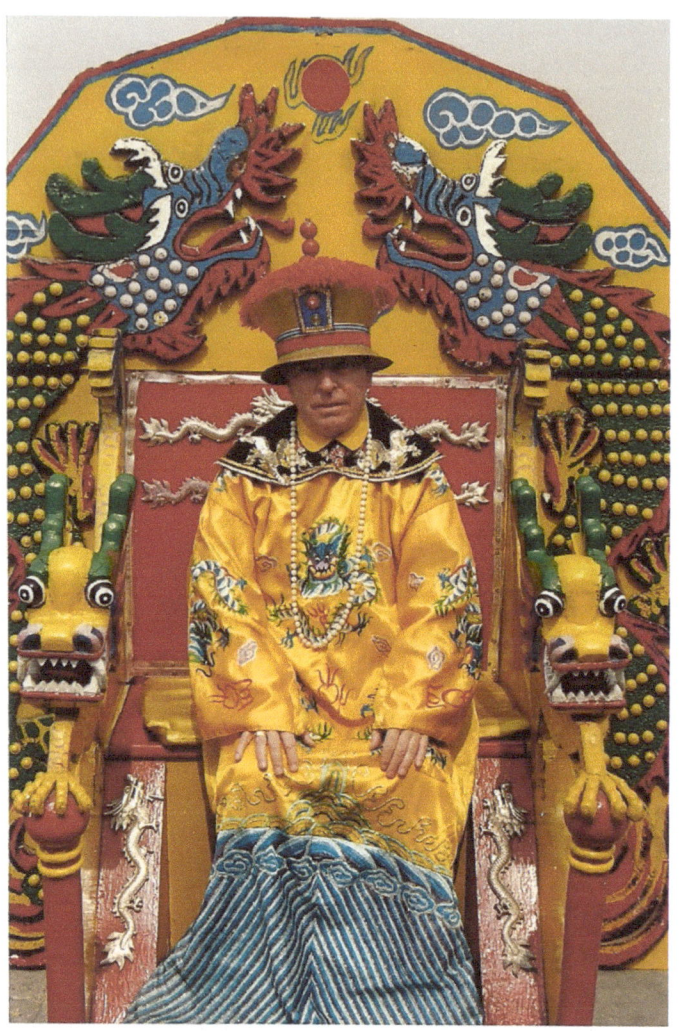

EMPEROR OF CHINA
MY REIGN LASTED ONLY
TILL THE SHUTTER CLICKED
SHORTEST IN THE HISTORY
OF CHINA

WALL

LEARN FROM HISTORY
OR YOU WILL REPEAT IT
THE WALL BETWEEN COUNTRYS
HAS NEVER WORKED
AND NEVER WILL
THERE ARE BETTER WAYS

NATIVE AMERICANS WELCOMED
THE EUROPEANS SEEKING A
BETTER LIFE AWAY FROM THE
SUPPRESSIONS DICTATED
THEY DID NOT BUILD A WALL
AMERICA WAS ENRICHED

WE CALL THIS IMMIGRATION
THE GOING LAWS DICTATE
THAT OUR BOARDERS MUST
BE SECURE AND ILLEGAL'S
REMAIN IN PLACE TILL THEY
MEET THE COUNTRIES STANDARDS

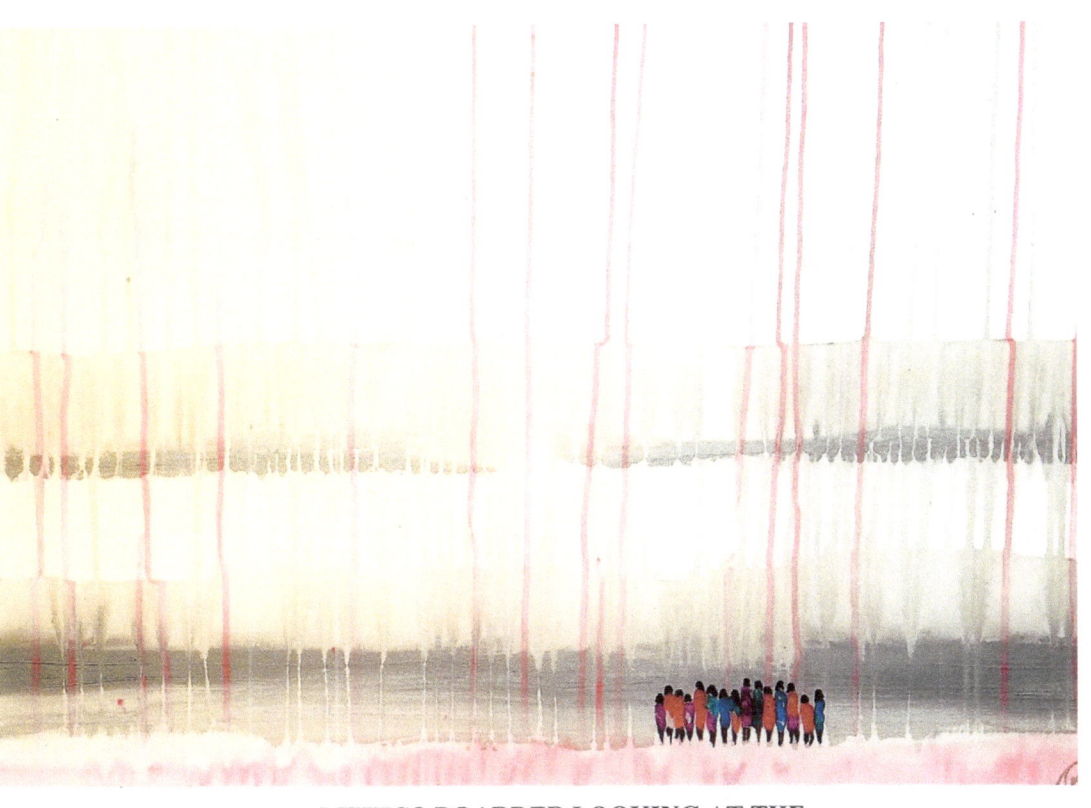

MEXICO BOARDER LOOKING AT THE
RIO GRANDE AND THE AMERICAN WALL

ANCIENT CHINA BUILT THE GREAT
WALL TO PROTECT THE BOARDER
AGAINST THE MONGOLIANS TO THE NORTH
GENGHIS KHAN AND HIS HORDES
BREECHED IT, HEADED SOUTH AS FAR
AS BEIJING AND OTHER AREAS
HOW THE DID IT, IS STILL A MYSTERY
THEORY THAT GATE GUARDS WERE BRIBED
BUILT WITH LOSS OF LIFE AND
UNIMAGINABLE COST THIS MAGNIFICENT
WALL NEVER WORKED AS INTENDED
MOST OF WHATS LEFT
IS A TOURIST GEMSTONE

RUSSIA BUILD A WALL IN GERMANY
TO KEEP THE EAST GERMANS CONTAINED
FROM CROSSING OVER TO THE WEST
MANY FOUND WAYS TO CROSS FOR FREEDOM
THIS WALL WAS TORNED DOWN
A SHORT-LIVED WALL THAT NEVER WORKED

OUR CURRENT PRESIDENT IS BUILDING A WALL
TO SAFE GUARD OUR SOUTHERN BOARDERS
FROM CALIFORNIA TO TEXAS WHY
SAME OLD PROBLEM, MIGRANTS'
THEY JUST WANT A BETTER LIFE
AND AMERICA CAN GIVE IT TO THEM

THE STEEL COLUMN WALL 30' HIGH
IS COSTING BILLIONS I AM SURE
MUCH MORE WHEN ITS FINISHED
MEXICO WAS SUPPOSED TO PAY FOR IT
THEY NEVER WILL TO THIS DAY

EVEN WITH ALL OF THE GUARDS
AND HIGH-TECH EQUIPMENT
ALL YOU NEED IS A STEEL CUTTING
TORCH TO MAKE A PASSAGE
OR TUNNEL UNDER THE FOUNDATIONS
OR MANY OTHER WAYS
HISTORY REPEATS IT SELF

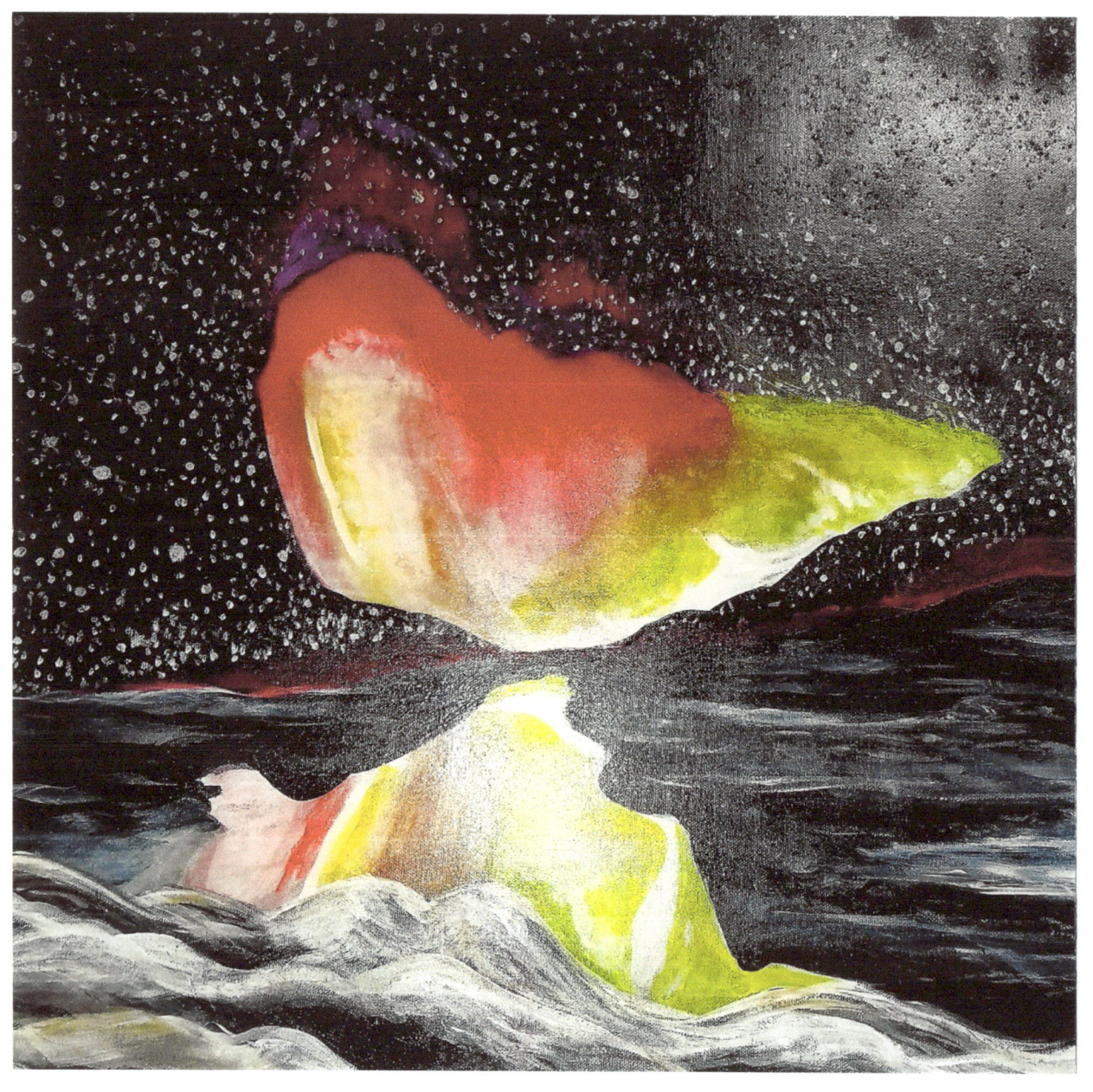

DANCING
NORTHERN
LIGHTS
WITH THE
LAKE
AS A
PARTNER

44

LANCE & LAURA

IN KENYA

OUR TIME IN LONDON CAME TO AN END
LANCE, SHE ASKED WHERE DO WE GO
THINKING AFRICA LET'S TALK ABOUT IT
IT'S A COUNTRY DEVIDED LIKE THE USA
DIFFERENCE IS EACH STATE
IS A COUNTRY OF ITS OWN
WAR AND STARVATION IN MANY A STATE
I THINK WE CAN TO AND RECORD
THE HUMAN PLIGHT

FOR OPENERS LETS PICK A PEACEFUL PLACE
FOR US TO CAPTURE ITS NATURE
THE HUMAN AND WILD LIFE EXPERIENCE
LET'S GO TO KENYA AND SO THEY WENT
FROM HEATHROW THERE IT WAS
A VERY LONG FLIGHT
THEY TALKED ABOUT THEIR LIVES
JUST TO BETTER UNDER UNDERSTAND
THEIR DOMESTIFICATION

WE ARE LANDING IN KENYA
SOME CITY THAT I HOPED THE PILOT NEW
CUSTOMS WAS A BREEZE ONLY ONE GUARD
AN AK-47 RESTED IN HIS ARMS DRESSED IN TAN SHORTS
IT WAS AFRICAN STYLE CITY
THEY DID HAVE AN AIRPORT
WE ASKED THE GREETORS FOR
WHO WOULD GIVE US A RIDE?
TO THE BEST HOTEL IN THE CITY
THE SIGN STATED WECOME TO
NAIROBI IT WAVED IN THE WIND
WE COULD THEN PLAN WHERE TO GO

THIS 6 STAR HOTEL ROOMS TO DELIGHT
HIGH TEA AT THREE, THE BAR NEVER CLOSES
SHOWER AND RESTED, PLANS DISCUSSED AT DINNER
LET'S TAKE A FEW DAYS, SEE THE CITY
THE ENGLISH WERE HERE THEY LEFT IN 63

FIRST DAY ON A WALK HIS CAMERA READY
LAURA WITH HER TAPE RECORDER
SHE HAD GIVEN UP THE PENCIL AND PAD
HER THOUGHTS WERE FASTER
LANCE OBSERVED THAT ENGLAND
IN HISTORY WANTED ALL OF COLLEGES
TO COLLECT AND CHANGE TO THEIR
WAY OF LIFE, OFTEN THROWEN OUT
SOMETIMES LEAVE IN THE DARK OF NIGHT
THEIR INFLUENCE WAS STILL THERE
THEY AGREED NAIROBI HAD ENGLISH CHARM

WHEN THE FEW DAYS WERE UP
ITS TIME TO FOLLOW OUR GAME PLAN
THEY ARE MANY PROTECTED PARKS
THAT ARE VERY CLOSE, WILD LIFE AND NATURE
LET'S TALK TO AN AGENT ONE THAT KNOWS
FOR A SMALL FEE THAT WERE ONLY THREE
THIS OUTFITTER IS THE BEST
FOR ALL THE PARKS LET ME ARRANGE
YOUR TRAVEL ITINERARY
HE TOOK OUR PLASTIC WITH A SMILE

NEXT MORNING AT HALF PAST TEN
THE LAND ROVER APPEARED
A JOLLY BLACK GIANT LOADED OUR GEAR
MY NAME IS BOY AND I KNOW YOURS
WHEN WE ARE FRIENDS, I'LL TELL MY NAME
HE WAS A GOOD DRIVER
THROUGH NAIROBI STREETS WE FLEW
WE WERE TO LEARN HE ALSO A GUIDE
THE FIRST NORTHERN CAMP
WE COULD NOT BELIEVE
A SIGN READ HIGH TEA AT THREE

THEY HAD EVERYTHING TO MEET OUR NEEDS
A LAP OF PURE LUXURY IN THE AFRICAN OUT BACK
THE FOOD AND WINE WERE HEAVEN DEVINE
THEY HAD THE BEST CHEFS AND STAFF
TO INTRODUCES TO NEW NEEDS
A DAY AFTER REST BOY CAME TO US
WHAT YOU LIKE TO SEE AND RECORD
EVERY THING HERE IS ABUNDANCE
HOWEVER, I KNOW THE BEST PLACES TO GO
WE THEN KNEW WE WERE IN GOOD HANDS

TOMORROW WE LEAVE
BEFORE DOWNS EARLY LIGHT
THE LAND ROVER WAS NEW
BOY AND BOY2 HAD RIFLES WITH NO SCOPES
I ASKED WHY NO SCOPES BOY LAUGHED
THEY ARE FOR OUR PROTECTION
INCASE WE BECOME THE PREY
WE WILL KNOW WHEN THEY GET TO CLOSE
LINE OF SIGHT THREW IRON SIGHTS
WORKS THE BEST AT LAST RESORT

I SURVEYED THE ROVER AND HAD NO SURPIZE
IT WAS LOADED WITH FOOD, WATER AND GAS
TWO PAIR OF BINOCULARS SO WE ALL COULD SEE
IN THE NEXT FEW DAYS BOY TOOK US
TO PLACES UNTOUCHED AND NATURAL
MY CAMERA WAS FULL SO I DOWN LOADED
LAURA HAD AN ENDLESS SUPPLY OF TAPES
WE WERE BOTH CHILDREN IN A CANDY STORE
WILD LIFE AND NATURE WE WERE GLAD TO BE HERE

IN A FEW WEEKS WE NEW THE COUNTRY WELL
WE ASKED BOY AND BOY2 TO STAY
IN THE CAMP BUT LOAD THE ROVER
SAME AS BEFORE AND LAURA WOULD DRIVE
BOYS ONLY WORDS DON'T GO TO FAR
AND BE CAREFUL IT HAD RAINED THE DAY BEFORE
LAURA AND I JUST WANTED TO BE ALONE
JUST US ONES IN NATURAL BEAUTY
MAYBE JUMP IN THE BACK SEAT
WE HAD ENDED PLATONIC
A LONG TIME AGO

THE MORNING AIR WAS HUMID BUT COOL
LAURA HIT PEDAL TO THE METAL
OFF WE WENT NO DUST TO FOLLOW
SHE DIRECTED THE ROVER
TO HER VERY SPECIAL PLACE
SUNLIGHT AND MORNING DEW
ON THE LEAVES OF THE TREES
LITTLE DID WE KNOW WHAT WAS TO FOLLOW
IF WE DID IT WOULD NOT BE ADVENTURE

AFRICAN NAME FOR ARROYO OR GULLY
TWO FEET DEEP IN MUD ALL FOUR WHEELS SUNK
SPINING AND SLIDING AND SLINGING MUD
DRY LAND A FEW FEET AWAY
WITH A BIG TRUNK TREE, I WAS GLAD TO SEE
LAURA SAID IT'S TIME TO USE THE WENCH
LANCE GET AND JUMP FROM THE HOOD
GRAB THE CABLE AND HOOK AND TIE TO THE TREE
YOU WON'T BELIEVE WHAT I WAS DESTINE TO SEE
I DID AS SHE ASKED AND BEFORE I COULD TIE IT
LOOKED UP IN THE TREE

ABOUT HALF WAY UP, WAS A YELLOW TAIL
SWING IN THE BREEZE, BETWEEN THE LEAVES
DRAPED IN A FORK WAS A BODY YELLOW
WITH BLACK POAKADOTS IN NO PATTERN
A BEAUTYFUL HEAD WAS LOOKING AT ME
COLD BLACK EYES WITH WHITE WISKERS
TELEACOMMUNICATION NO WORD SPOKEN
CLIMB THE TREE AND VIST WITH ME

MY MOTHERS ADVISE CAME TO ME
BUT I WAS DRAWN LIKE A MAGNET
HAND AND FOOT, I CLIMBED THE TREE
REST IN THE LOWER FORK AND LOOK AT ME
I DON'T OPEN INVITE STRANGERS
YOU'RE THE EXCEPTION I FELT NO FEAR
I LOVE SEATING HERE BY THE WADI
AND WATCHING THE ON GOING
HUMAN CIRCUS MAKES ME LAUGH A LOT

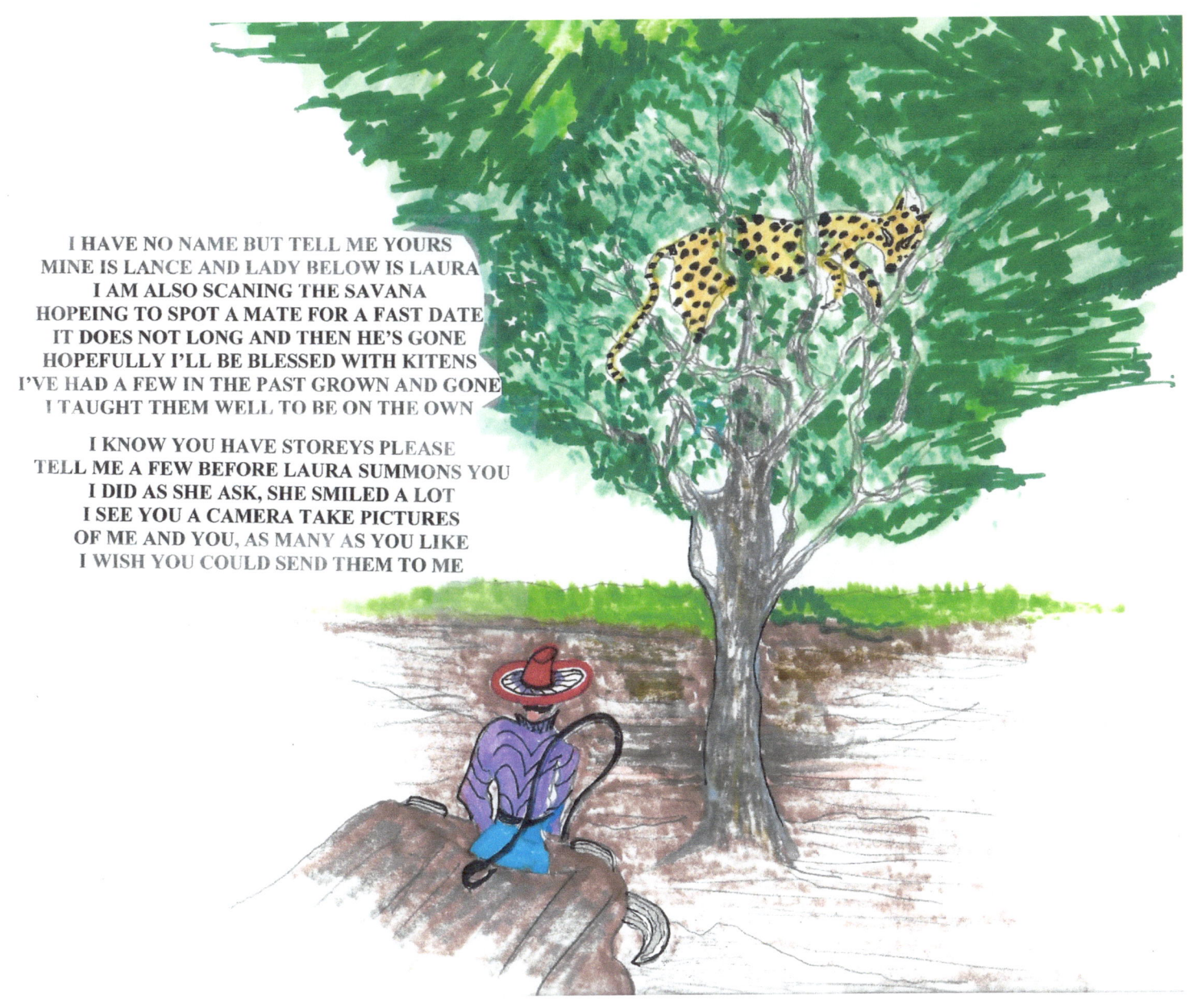

I HAVE NO NAME BUT TELL ME YOURS
MINE IS LANCE AND LADY BELOW IS LAURA
I AM ALSO SCANING THE SAVANA
HOPEING TO SPOT A MATE FOR A FAST DATE
IT DOES NOT LONG AND THEN HE'S GONE
HOPEFULLY I'LL BE BLESSED WITH KITENS
I'VE HAD A FEW IN THE PAST GROWN AND GONE
I TAUGHT THEM WELL TO BE ON THE OWN

I KNOW YOU HAVE STOREYS PLEASE
TELL ME A FEW BEFORE LAURA SUMMONS YOU
I DID AS SHE ASK, SHE SMILED A LOT
I SEE YOU A CAMERA TAKE PICTURES
OF ME AND YOU, AS MANY AS YOU LIKE
I WISH YOU COULD SEND THEM TO ME

47

I DID AS SHE ASKED A SELFIE OF ME AND HER
LAURA BECOMED ME GET DOWN FROM THE TREE
WE HAVE TO SET THE ROVER FREE
RELUCKTANTLY I START DOWN
WITH FOND FARE WELL TO
THE LADY LEOPARD IN THE TREE
I TIED THE CABLE TO THE TREE
LAURA STARTED THE WENCH
THE ROVER CAME FREE

ON THE OTHER SIDE AND IN DRY LAND
LAURA ASKED WHY DID YOU CLIMB THE TREE
I SHOW YOU REASON ITS IN MY CAMERA
I HIT THE MODE THAT WOULD SHOW
ALL IMAGES WITH MY COMPLETE SURPRIZE
ALL THAT WAS THERE WERE SELFIES OF ME
I COULD NOT BELIEVE WAS IT A FANTASY
LAURA TURN YOUR RECORDER ON
AND I WILL TELL YOU THE STOREY

SHE WAS DASILED BEYOUND BELIIEVE
IT WILL BE A CHAPTER IN MY BOOK
TIME FOR LUNCH I DID BRING BEER
AS WE ATE AND RESTED A THOUGHT
VERY STRONG CAME TO ME
LAURA LET'S JUMP IN THE BACK SEAT
WHOLE HEARTLY SHE AGREED

IT WAS EARLY AFTERNOON IT WAS TIME
TO RETURN TO BASE CAMP LET'S CIRCLE AROUND
ALL WADI'S NO MATTER IF THEY LOOK DRY
WE HAD NOT VENTURED FAR TO BOYS DELIGHT
IT WAS TIME FOR A SHOWER AND DINNER
WHILE WE DRINKING CHAPAGNE WHEN BOY APPEARED
FOR LAST NUMBER WEEKS WE BECAME FRIENDS
NOW I WILL GIVE MY REAL NAME MY PROMISE TO KEEP
WE WAITED IN ANTISCIPATION HE SAID BOY1

THE STAFF NEW WE WERE LEAVING
BUT THEY HAD NO TIME OR DATE
SNUGGLING IN BED LAURA ASKED ME
LANCE WHERE DO WE GO NEXT
I HOPE ITS NOT LONDONS SNOW
OR KENYAS TROPICAL HEAT
WHERE EVER TED SENDS US
THAT'S ALL I KNOW

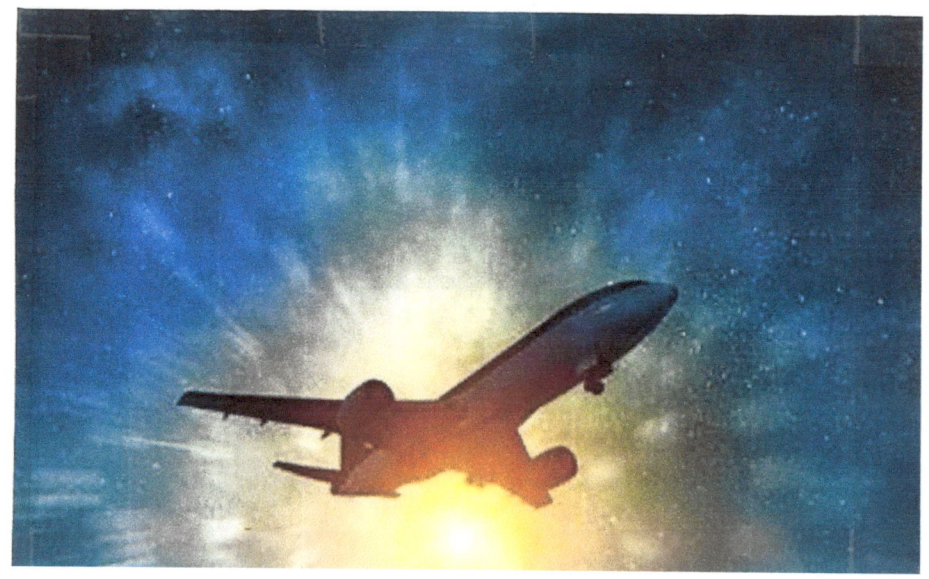

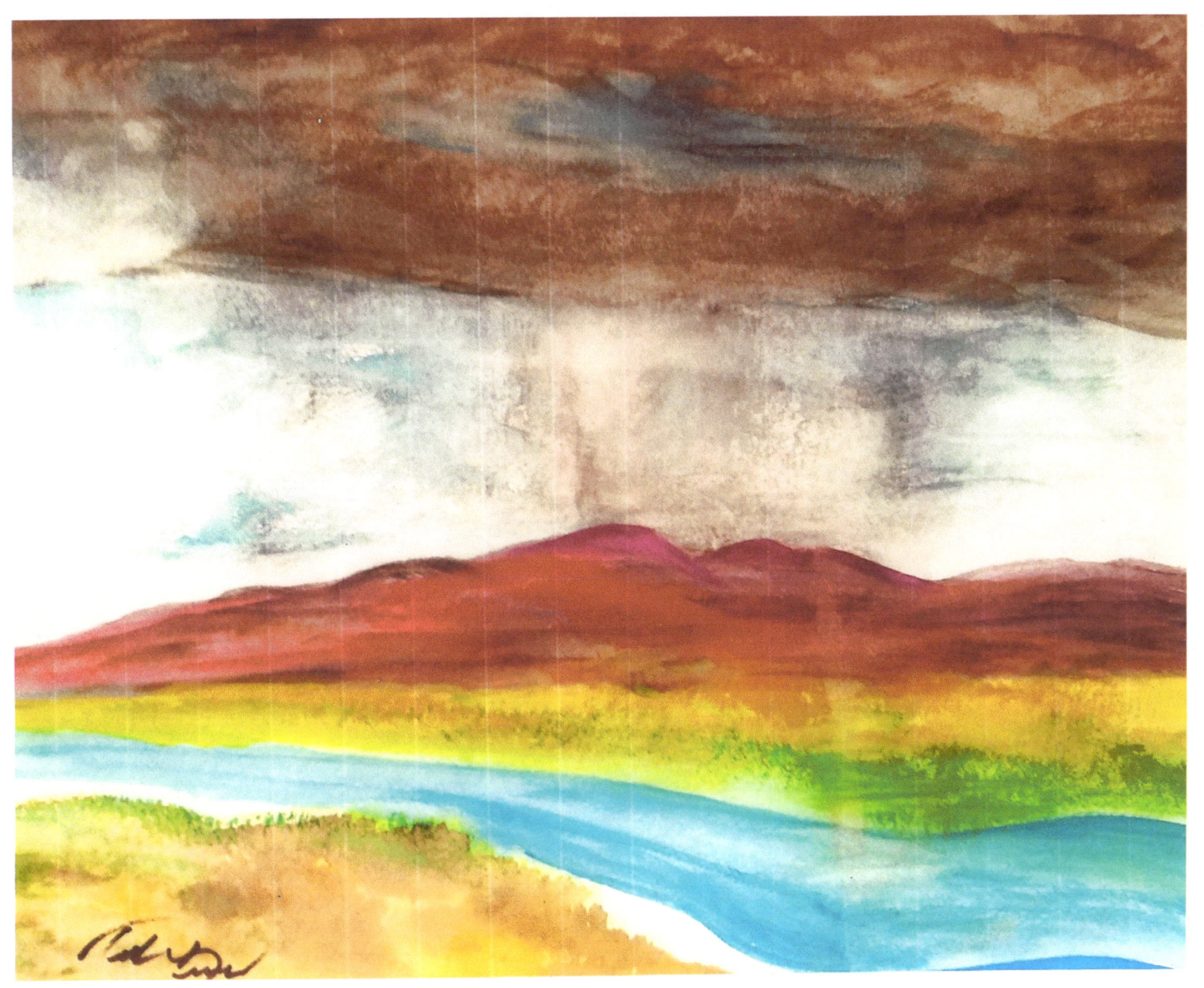

49

SURREAL SUN RISE
ALONG THE RIO GRANDE
IN NORTHERN NEW MEXICO

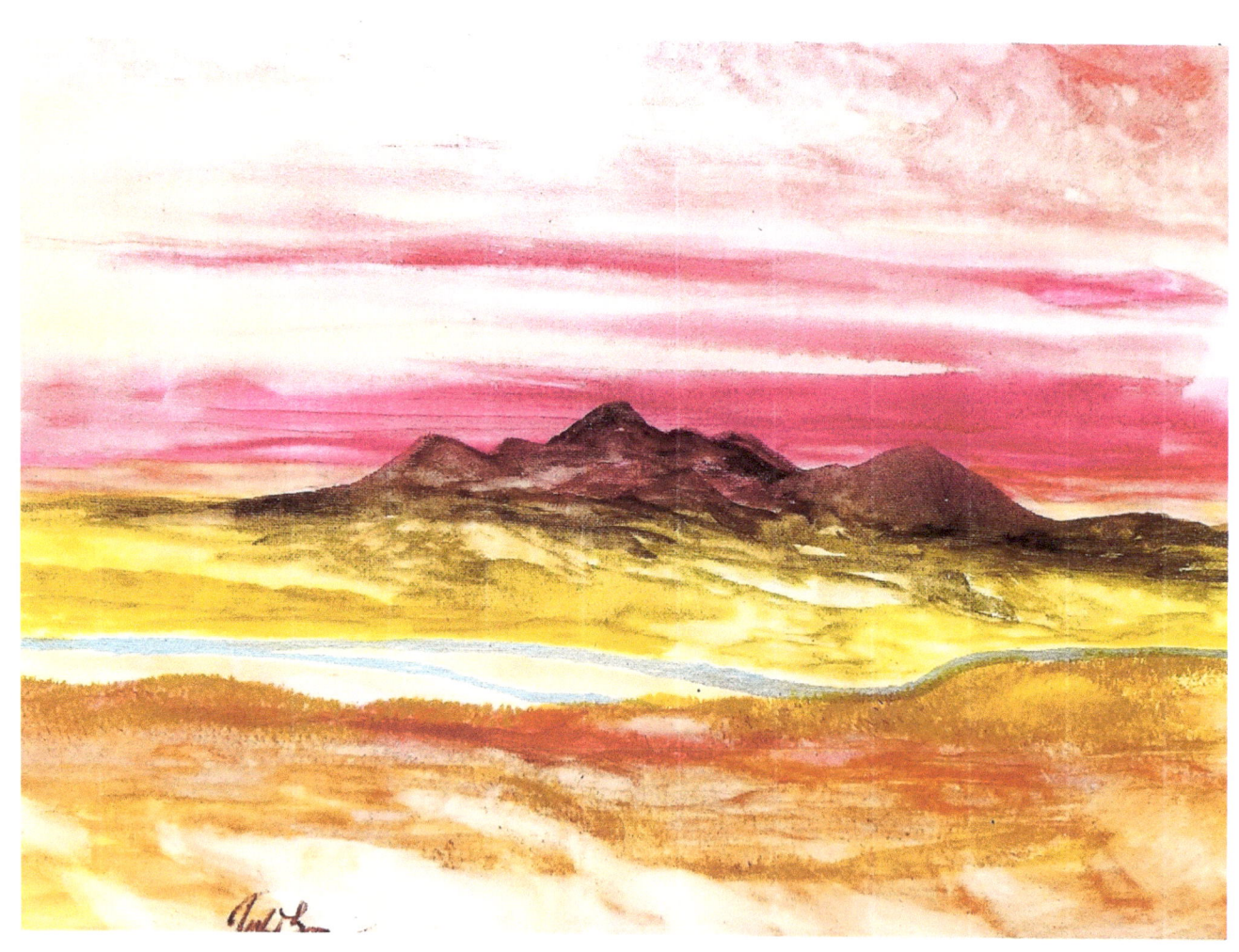

Memorial Day

Boots well worn
Long ago to tight
To twilight time
you still march in line
Rest will come
you know not where
Final rest never to be
Your are in the infantry

Fly! Fly! birdmen of the sky
Higher faster
Ever then before
Eagles here never soar
Seeing our world
The wing man turns
For you been in space
For which you were graced

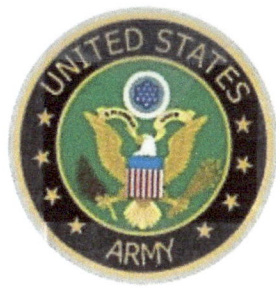
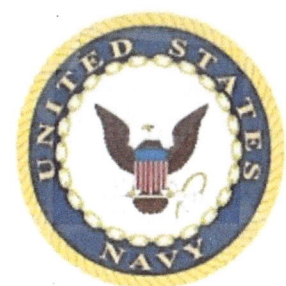
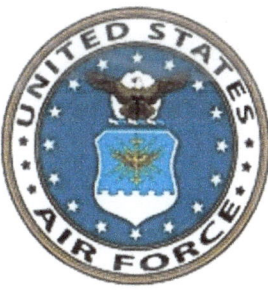
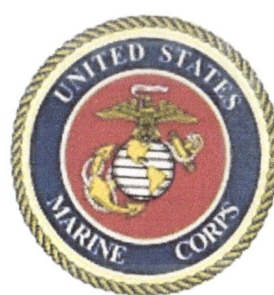

The color blue
Ships on the sea
Racing the waves
Shoreline never to see
Air is salty
Coating your spirit
The course is set
Much to your regret
It takes you from home
Sailor of destiny

Starting long ago
Marines you were called
Special guardians
With es-spirit dé corps
Proud as men can be
Your title for life
First to appear
Last to leave
History unraveled
Legacy decreed

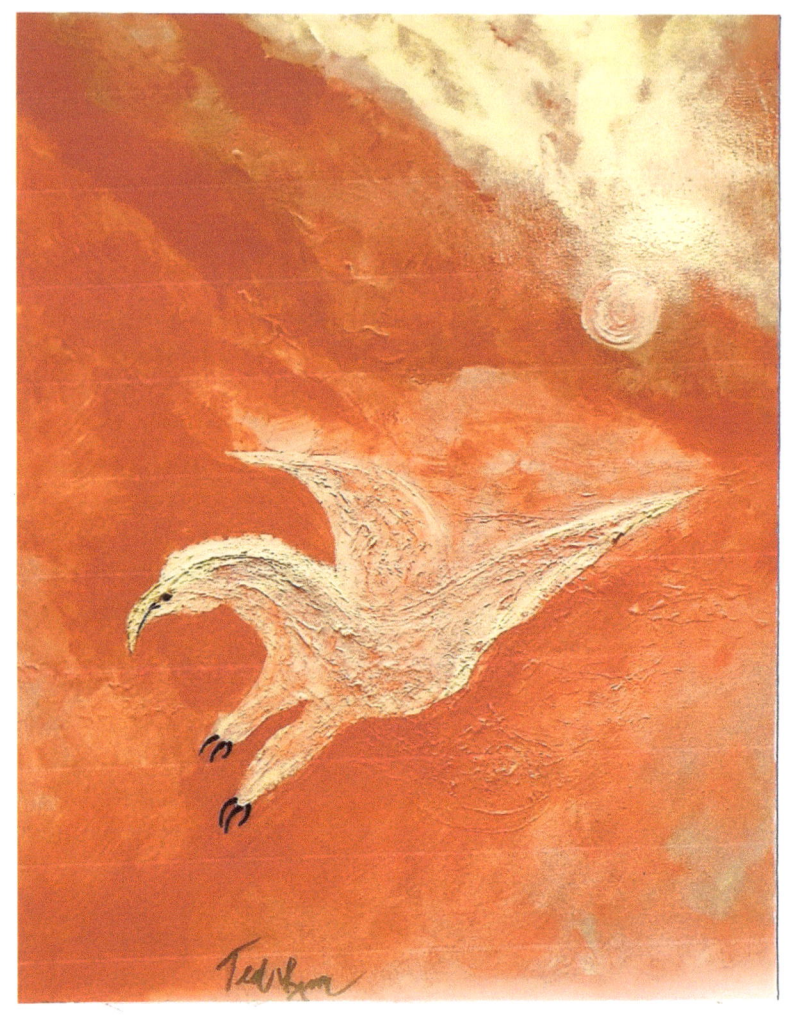

THE AMERICAN SPIRIT

EAGLE

THE EAGLE SOARS INSIDE HIMSELF FIRST
HE CONTEMPLATES ALL AROUND HIM
WITH THE INTENSITY OF KNOWING
HOW ABSOLUTELY MARVELOUS HE IS

HIS WINGS POINT THE WAY
AND HE SOARS ALWAYS KNOWING
THE BEST IS WHO HE IS
EXPERIENCING THE FLIGHT

FREEDOM TO MOVE IN HIS DIRECTION
WHERE THE REALITY OF HIS MIND
AND SPIRIT ARE COMBINED TO LIFT
HIM ABOVE HIS OWN BELIEF

THE EAGLE SOARS IN FREEDOM
AMONG THE EARLY MORNING FOG
HIS SPIRIT DESTING UNLOCKED
LOOKING AT THE SKY
AND MOTHER EARTH

THEODORO CORONA LUNA

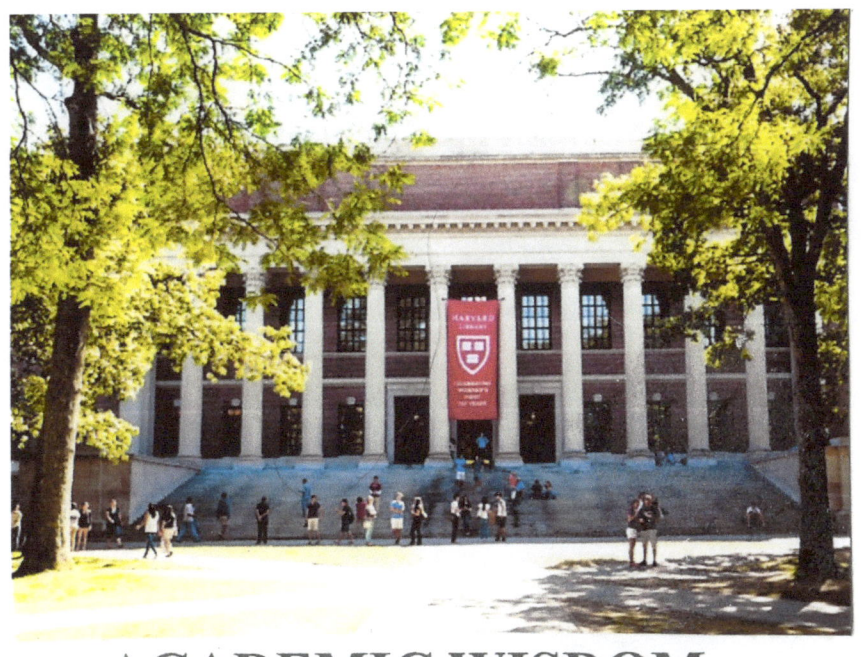

ACADEMIC WISDOM

AN NEWLY ANNOTED COLLEGE PROFESSOR
AT A PRESTIGES EASTERN UNIVERSITY
SET IN HIS OFFICE ON THE FIRST DAY
I THINK TO HIM SELF I SHOULD
SEEK THE COUNCIL AND ADVISE
OF THE MOST REVERED AND
TENURED PROFFESSOR HERE
AT THE UNIVERSITY

IN HIS RESEARCH HE KNEW WHO HE WAS
HE MADE AN APPOINTMENT WITH HIM
FOR THE FOLLOWING MORNING
OF COURSE, HE ARRIVED IN HIS BEST SUIT
AFTER INTRODUCTIONS AND HAND SHAKE
HE MOTIONED ME TO SIT IN A SOFT LEATHER COUCH
AND HE TOOK A WORN OUT CHAIR TO THE SIDE

CONGRADULATIONS WAS HIS FIRST WORDS
HOW CAN I HELP YOU?
I CAME FOR YOUR ADVICE AND WISDOM
SO, I MAY FORWARD TO A GREAT FUTURE
BUT MOST OF ALL TO ENDOW MY
STUDENTS WITH THE BEST EDUCATION POSSIBLE
A NOBLE GOAL FOR ALL ENERATIONS
PLEASE LET ME BEGIN ASK QUESTIONS
WHEN I CAN CLEAR A POINT

THERE ARE NO FIRSTS, SECONDS AND THIRDS
YOUR "F" FAILING STUDENTS WILL LEAVE
SOME WILL COME BACK, OTHERS
INTER THEIR OWN WORLD OF CHOOSING
THEIR MINDS WERE NEVER HERE
SOME ARE FIRST HERE BECAUSE OR PARENTS
OR FOR MANY OTHER REASONS
BUT ALL STUDENTS LOVE THE WORLD
OF COLLEGE PARTYS AND SPORTS

NO, YOU HAVE NOT FAILED
REMEMBER YOU CANNOT MAKE
A FISH CLIMB A MOUNTAIN
OR TURN THE UNIVERSE
UP SIDE DOWN

YOUR "D" STUDENTS ARE BOARDER LINE
YOUR COURSE MATERIAL MAY NOT INTEREST THEM
OR THEY ARE THERE BECAUSED ITS REQUIRED
OR IT HAS NOTHING TO DO WITH THEIR GOALS
IT SOON WILL DAWN ON THEM THE EFFECT
IT WILL HAVE ON THEIR GPA
SOME WILL TAKE THE COURSE OVER
AS FREASHMEN THE LIGHT WILL SOON
LIGHT AND NEXT YEAR WILL BE A
NEW BEGINNING IN ADDITUDE AND
MIND SET

YOUR "C" STUDENTS WILL GO OUT
AND CHANGE THE WORLD
AND MAKE IT A BETTER PLACE
FOR THE HUMAN EXPERIENCE
OFTEN ITS NOT BASED ON
THEIR COLLEGE DEGREE
IN A FIELD OF KNOWLEDGE
AS STATED ON THEIR WALL PAPER
BE VERY KIND TO THEM FOR THEY
RETURN AND GIVE YOU
10 MILLION DOLLARS FOR
NEW ADDITION

YOUR "B" STUDENTS WILL GO OUT
AND BECOME VERY PROFESSIONAL
SOME WILL BECOME ICONS
AND MOST WILL WORK VERY WELL
IN MOST AREAS AS DETERMINED
BY THE WORDS STATED ON THEIR
WALL PAPER IN MOST CASES
THEY ARE THE DRIVING FORCE
IN THEIR PROFFSSIONS
MOST OFTEN THEY WILL RESERCH
NEW IDEAS AND WAYS TO
ENHANCE ALL FACETS OF THE WORLDS
NEW AND SALEINT HUMAN EXPEIENCES
BY CHANGING MINDS AND APPROACHES
TO HELP RESOLVE OLD PROBEMS
AND IN SOME CASES
CREAT NEW ONES

YOUR "A" STUDENTS SOME WILL GO
AND THE BEST WILL STAY
IN THEIR FIELD OF ENDEVER
AT OUR UNIVERSITY OR OTHERS
THEY WILL BECOME COLLEAGUES
PROFESSORS, RESEARCHERS
BOOK PUBLISHERS AND MOST
OTHER FIELDS A UNIVERSITY
HAS TO OFFER
SOME WILL BE SITTING ON THE
COUCH YOUR SITTING ON
OFTEN THEY WILL CONTINUE THEIR
HIGHER EDUCATION OF
MASTERS AND PHD'S
IN MOST CASES THEY
CAN CHANGE THINKING IN
WAYS AND MEANS TO MAKE
OUR PLANET A BETTER
PLACE TO EXPERIENCE LIFE

YOUR ABOUT TO LIVE AND
EXPERIENCE THOUGHTS AND
EMOTIONS OF OTHER PEOPLES LIFES
WE CALL THEM STUDENTS
THE CAMPUS IS THE BEST HUNTING
GROUND FOR MATING
A VERY FEW WILL OFFER
THEIR BODYS FOR A PASSING GRADE
IT WILL BE A MORAL ISSUE FOR YOU
MORALLITY IS A VERY PERSONAL CHOICE
NO ONE HAS THE RIGHT TO QUESTION IT
THE BEST ADVISE I CAN GIVE YOU IS
PUBLISH OR YOU WILL PERISH
BE KIND, UNDERSTANDING AND COMPASSIONET
NOT ONLY TO YOUR STUDENTS BUT
TO EVERYONE THAT TOUCHEDES YOUR LIFE
AND SO IT IS
THE YOUNG PROFFESSOR STOOD UP
AND SAID WITH TEARS IN HIS EYES
SO BE IT

HAPPY BIRTHDAY
STEPHENIE

FLOWERS COME AND GO
SOME WORDS REMAIN
YOU ARE A JOY FOR LIFE
ARCHANGELS' COME TO EARTH
IN YOUR BEAUTY TO BEHOLD
COMPASSION IS YOUR BEING
LOVE AND UNDERSTANDING
CARING AND PATIENCE
ARE YOUR GIFT
TO OUR WORLD TO SEE
NUMBERS ARE THE COUNTERS
FORGET THEM ALL
FOR THE SPIRIT IS ALL
THAT IS THE DAILY
COUNTER THAT MATTERS
TO INSURE A WONDERFUL
MEANINGFUL LIFE
THESE ARE THE TRUE
TREASURES YOU GIVE TO ALL
THE UNIVERSE SENT ME A
DAUGHTER
SWEETHEART I AM SO GLAD
IT WAS YOU

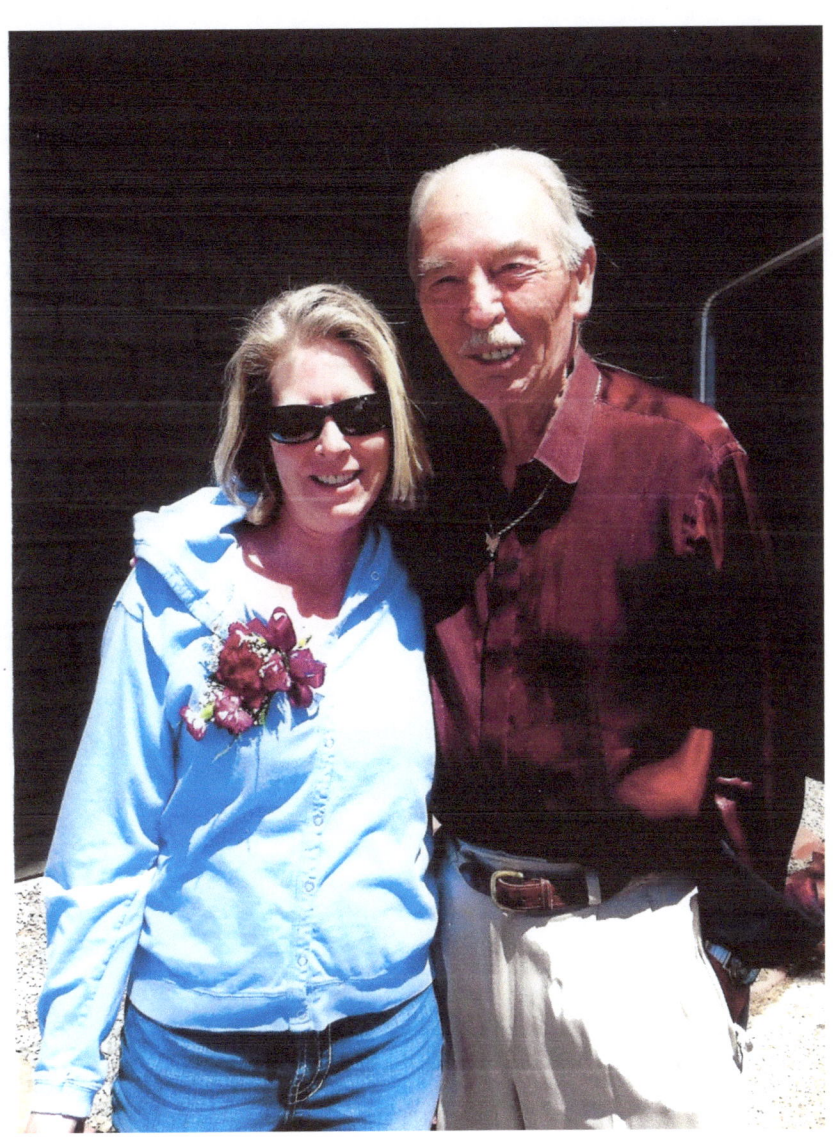

ARROW

BENDING MY HOME MADE
LEMON WOOD BOW
SECURED BY MY HEART STRINGS
I REACH OVER MY SHOLDER
TO THE SATIN RED LINNED
QUIVER HELD BY A
LEATHER STRAP AROUND
MY BOSSUM
I LIGHTLY FETCH MY ARROW
IT HAS NO FEATHERS
IT'S MY LASER GUIDED ARROW
I TOUCH MY RIGHT
CHEEK WITH FINGERS THREE
AND LET IT FLY
WHERE IT WILL LAND
I WISHED IT WELL
THROUGH THE COLD
CRISP MOUNTAIN AIR
A FLIGHT DEVINE
CUPID'S STUPID ARROW
A FANTASY AT BEST
TARGETS THE ONES LOOKING
FOR ENDLESS LOVE
MY ARROW WILL FIND HER
AND GIVE ME THE PATH
BLOND, AUBURN, RED OR BLACK
BEAUTIFUL IN SPIRIT
BODY PARTS ASUNDER
FREEDOM TO EXPLORE
THE WOUNDER OF BEING
O LASER GUIDED ARROW
WHERE IS SHE

ON THE ARCHERY RANGE OAHU

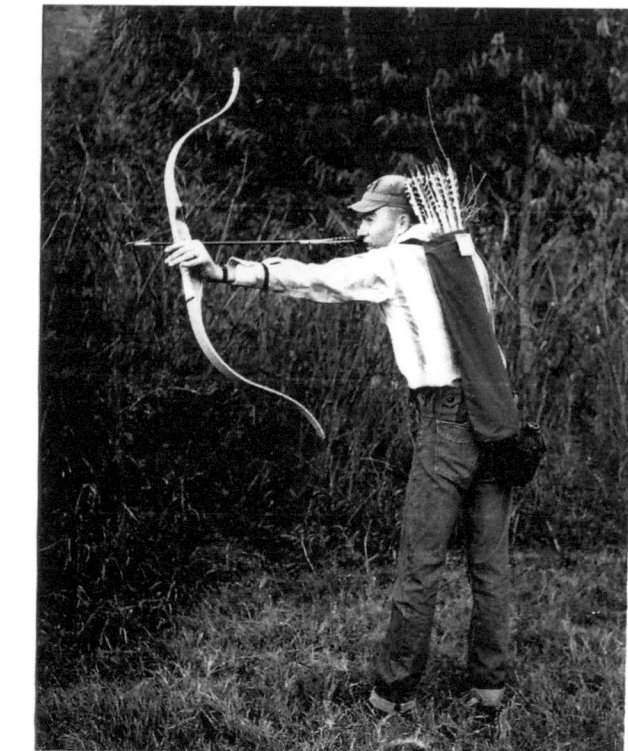

THE BOW, ARROWS AND QUIVER WERE MADE BY ME.
OFF DUTY WITH A FEW FRIENDS THAT TAUGHT ME.
THE 10 TARGET COURSE HAD UPS AND DOWNS CLOSE BY
TO BARBERS POINT NAVEL AIR STATION. WE WOULD
CHANGE THE TARGET POINTS TO BROAD HEADS ON THE
ARROWS TO GO FOR BOW HUNTING ON THE BIG ISLAND
OF HAWAII. WE FLEW TO THE HILO AIRPORT IN OUR
TWO ENGINE SNB GENERALLY PRETTY ROUGH RIDE.
WE HEAD TO PARKER RANCH LOCATED IN THE LUSH
VALLEY BETWEEN THE MOUNTAINS OF MAUNA KEA
AND MANUNA LOA FOR A FEW DAYS HUNT. THE GAME
WERE WILD PIGS AND GOATS. FIRST NIGHT AFTER
A FEW DRINKS WE ALL AGREED NEVER TO KILL
ONLY TO FIND AND SHOOT THE ARROWS FOR A MISS.
NO ONE BROKE THE VOW AND AS ALLWAYS WE HAD
FUN. ONLY PROBLEM WAS TRY TO WASH OUR BOOTS
FROM THE BLACK LAVA BEDS DUST.

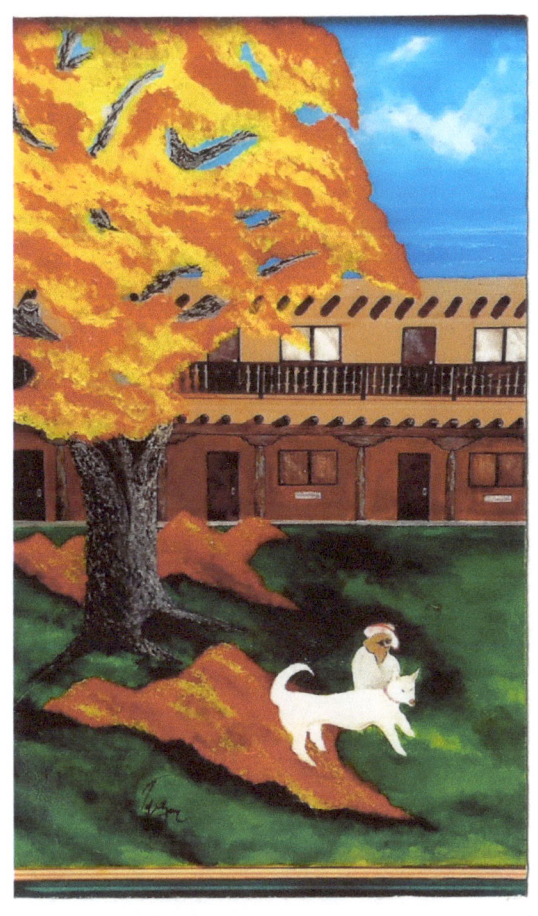

SAGEBURSH INN TAOS
NEVER MET THE LADY
WE ENJOYED THE STAY

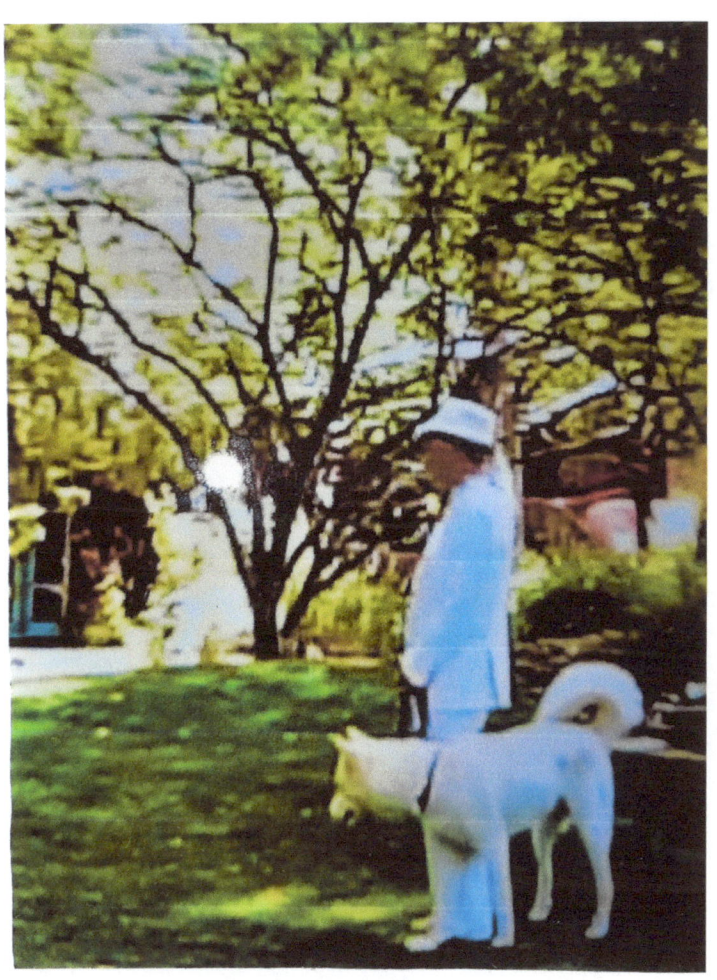

"A WHITE SILK SUIT WITH
NO PINK CARNATION"
DESTINY BLESSED
WAYNE AND PAT
DESTINY

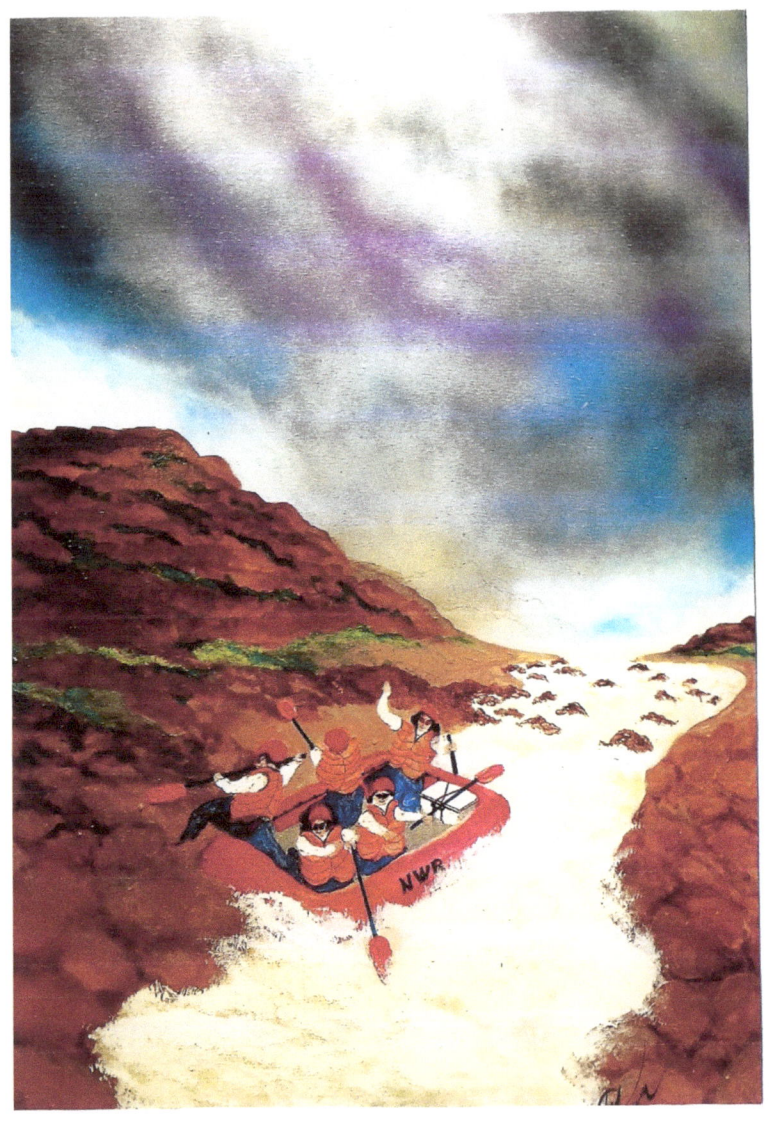

RAFTING ON THE RIO

ODE TO THE
RIO GRANDE
ON IT'S 1800 MILE JOURNEY

I STEPPED ACROSS A TWO FOOT
STREAM, HIGH UP IN COLORADO
SOUTHEREN ROCKY MOUNTAINS
FED BY ARTESIAN BUBBLES
NEAR A VILLAGE I CAN'T REMEMBER
THE BIRTH PLACE OF THE RIO

I STEPPED ACROSS A TWO FOOT
STREAM HIGH UP IN THE PECOS
WILDERNESS ON A HORSE PACK
TRIP, IT HAD NATIVE TROUT
THE BIRTH PLACE OF THE PECOS
RIVER IN NEW MEXICO

BOTH WOULD JOIN SOMEWHERE
TEXAS AND TOGETHER THEY
FLOW TO THE SALTY GULF
OF MEXICO AND FREASH WATER
FOREVER LOST AS THEY BECAME
ONE WITH THE GULF

THE RIO WATER WOULD HAVE
A TAPESTRY OF COLOR AND MOODS
FED BY MANY LESSOR STREAMS
RAIN, SNOW MELT, FLOOD CONTROL
RACING THROUGH DEEP CANYONS
BUT GENTLE ON FLAT LOW LANDS

MAN, IN HIS WISDOM CREATED DAMS
TO ENSURE WATER SUPPLY AND
MOST OF ALL MUCH-NEEDED LAKES
A GOD'S SEND TO THE ARID STATE
OF NEW MEXICO AND TEXAS
A JOY OF NEW RECREATION FOR ALL

LANCE & LAURA
MEXICO CLUB MED

OUT OF NAIROBI WE DID FLY
MANY CONNECTING WEIGHT STATIONS
FINALLY, THE LAST WAS TO SEE
THE BLUE ATLANTIC PASSED BELOW
THE PILOT WITH A MEXICAN TONE
WELCOME TO MEXICO WE LAND
IN CANCUN

I HAD MADE RESERVATIONS BY THE NET
WE WERE GOING TO HAVE A WEEK
OF REST AND FUN, CUSTOMS WAS A JOKE
AMONG THE GREETERS A MAN WITH A SIGN
CLUB MED WELCOMES LANCE AND LAURA
FOLLOW ME, TO THE SCHUTLE VAN
TWO OTHER COUPLES SET IN THE SEATS

WE WERE GREETED WITH A GLASS
WHAT IT CONTAINED I DARE NOT ASK
THE YOUNG HANDSOME MAN
BEHIND THE CHECK IN COUNTER
SMILED AT US, CHECKED HIS COMPUTER
I DON'T RECOMMEND THE UNITS BY THE SEA
THE WINDS ARE STRONG BUT
THE ONES AT THE LAGOON ARE
THE BEST PEACEFUL QUIET, SUN RISE TO SEE

THE UNITS WERE SIZED RIGHT WITH BALCONY
MUCH OUR SURPRISE ONLY TWO VERY SMALL BEDS
NO BIGGER THAN A ONE-MAN SLEEPING BAG
LAURA LAUGHED, LANCE WE WILL MAKE DO
THE TEMPERATURE AND THE OCEAN AIR
OF COURSE, AS AN ALL INCLUSIVE RESORT
THE HOSPITAL TYPE RIBBON ON OUR WRIST
WAS ALL WE NEEDED, NO SIGNING TABS EXIST

THE THREE NO WALL OPEN BAR
HAVE EVERY LIQUER SENT FROM A FAR
THE ONLY SCHEDULE THE TIME FOR
THE NORMAL THREE SQUARES A DAY
THE FOOD AND DRINK OF COURSE
WERE OUTSTANDING WE WOULD
SURELY GAIN WEIGHT OR SWIM IT AWAY

THE NEVER ENDING ACTIVITYS BY THE STAFF
DAILY WERE FUN WITH LATE EVENING SHOWS
NOT ON FLIM, THEATRE PRODUCTIONS
BY GUESTS AND STAFF
LAURA AND I ACTED IN THREE
ON THE NIGHT OF THE THIRD DAY
BEFORE BED I TOLD LAURA, A GOLF COURSE EXISTED
AT THE HILTON HOTEL A FEW MILES AWAY
I HAD LEARNED THE SPORT AT HARVARD
AND I WANTED TO PLAY, EVERYTHING I NEEDED
WOULD BE THE SWIPE OF PLASTIC

I ASKED LAURA IF SHE WANTED TO GO
SHE SAID NO BUT GO AND PLAY
SHE SAID SHE WOULD SPEND THE DAY
AT THE POOL ON A LOUNGE WITH DRINK IN HAND
TOP-LESS IN HER BIKINI LIKE EVERY ONE ELSE
I AM HOPING TO GET AN EVEN TAN
I WORK ON MY BOOK
AND TOMOROW HAVE A GREAT DAY

MEDS SHUTTLE VAN WAS FAST
THE GOLF COURSE APPEARED I CHECKED IN
THE CLUB HOUSE AND MET WITH THE PRO
HIS ASSISTANT FITTED ME
WITH ALL THAT I NEEDED ASSIGNED ME A CART
I WAS READY TO GO WITH WHOM I DID NOT KNOW
TWO OTHER FELLOWS FROM THE STATES
STATED THEY WERE PGA PROS
AFTER A GOOD START THEY LEFT ME FAR BEHIND
NOT EVEN A CHEERFUL GOODBYE
I WAS ALL ALONE FOR THE REST OF THE COURSE

OF WELL I HAVE PLAYED ALONE BEFORE
HOLE NUMBER 7 WAS A PAR 3
MY 9 IRON SHOT LANDED 5' FROM THE GREEN
AS I DROVE UP MY HEART TOOK A JUMP
THERE TWO FEET FROM THE GREEN
LAYED AN EIGHTEEN FOOT ALLIGATOR
SHOULD I LEAVE THE BALL AND
HEAD FOR THE NEXT TEE
AS HE OR SHE LIFTED THE HEAD
LOOKED ME STRAIGHT IN MY EYES
TELEAPATHIC COMMUNICATIONS
IN MY MIND AND HIS
HAVE NO FEAR THAT'S WHAT HE TOLD ME

COME SPEND A LITTLE TIME AND VIST WITH ME
I STEPPED DOWN FROM THE CART
MY CAMERA WAS ALWAYS READY
TOOK A FEW IMAGES OF THE HIM
INCLUDING THE GREEN
NEARLY A FEW FEET AWAY HE GAVE ME
AN MEXICAN ALLIGATOR HELLO
TEN FEET AWAY WAS A VERY LARGE LAGOON
MY NAME IS ALLI PLEASE TELL ME YOURS
LANCE, I SAID NICE TO MEET YOU

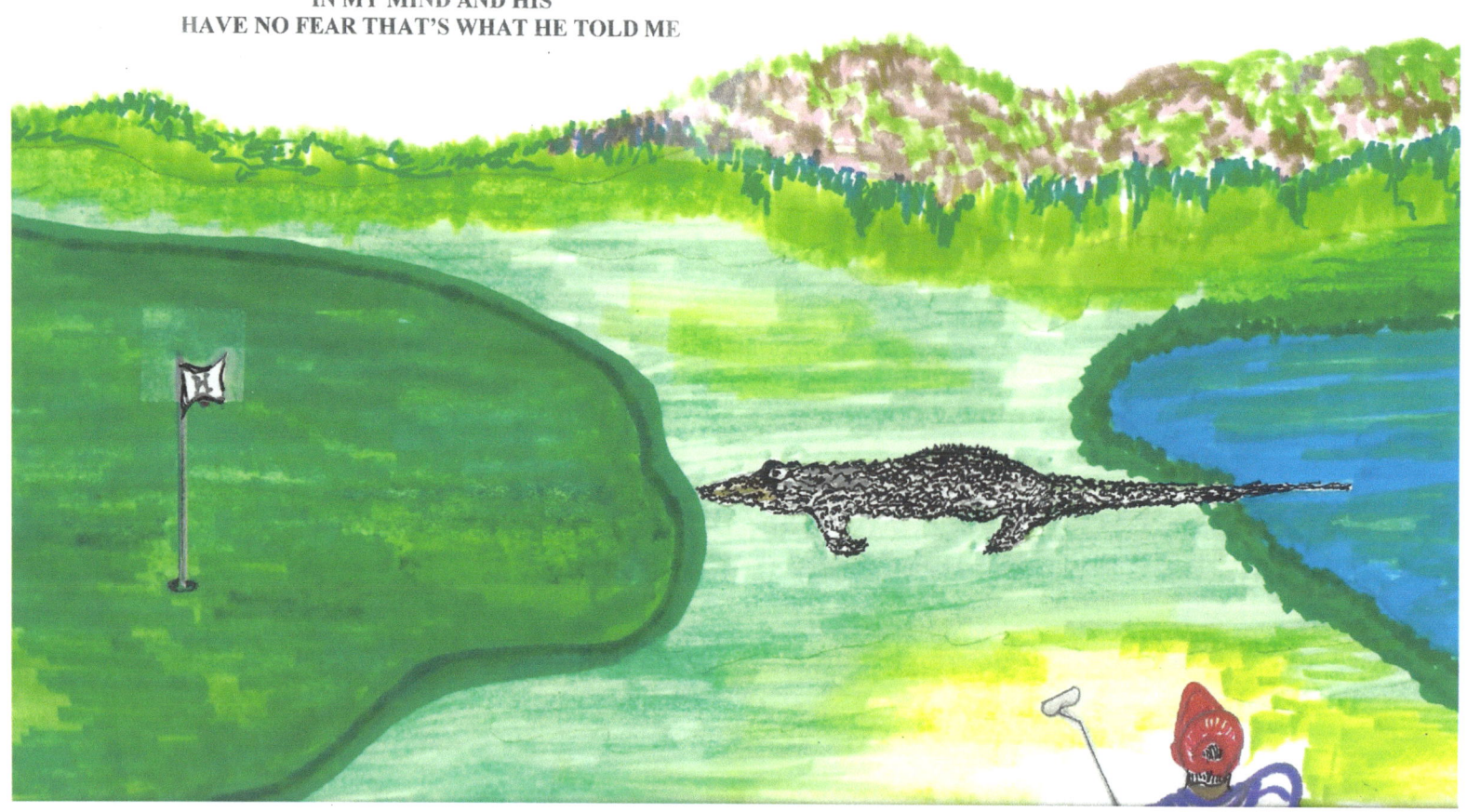

THE FUN I HAVE IS TO WATCH THE GOLFERS
JUST BEFORE YOU CAME, TWO GOLFERS
TOOK ONE LOOK AT ME, DID NOT STRIKE THE BALL
GUNNED THE CART TO THE NEXT TEE
I KNOW WHO THEY ARE PGA STARS
I AM NOW GLAD THEY LEFT ME FAR BEHIND
LET'S SHARE A FEW STORIES I'LL GO FIRST
I CAME HERE FIRST WHEN I WAS JUST 7' LONG
TAKE WITH A NOOSE AND VERY STRONG ARMS
MY BIRTH PLACE I'LL NEVER KNOW

THE KEEPERS HERE ARE VERY NICE
THEY FEED ME WHAT I CAN'T FINED IN THE LAGOON
THEY SOON BROUGHT ME A MATE
OF COURSE, WE HAD TO DATE
LONG BEFORE WE COULD MATE
AFTER A WHILE SHE DIED ON ME
THEY FOUND 50 GOLF BALLS SHE COULD
NOT DIGEST EATEN AT THE BOTTOM
OF THE DEEP LAGOON

THIS IS THE SADEST STORY I HAVE MANY MORE
IT'S YOUR TURN LANCE TELL ME A FEW
I ONLY RECITED THE HAPPY ONES I KNEW
PLEASE TAKE SOME SELFIES OF YOU AND ME
BECAUSE I'M GETTING READY TO TAKE A NAP
ALLI THEN I WILL GO AND SAY A FARWELL
TO ALLI MY MEXICAN ALLIGATOR
HOPPED ON THE CART TO THE CLUB HOUSE
I DID FEEL I COULD FINISH   THE REMAINING
ELEVEN HOLES

THE ASSISTANT WAS SURPRISED HE SAID TO ME
NO ONE HAS EVER PLAYED THIS COURSE THAT FAST
I DID NOT WANT TO EXPLAIN TURNED IN MY GEAR
SORRY SENIOR I CAN NOT GIVE YOU A REFUND
EVEN IF YOU ONLY PLAYED SEVEN
JUST PLEASE CALL ME A TAXI AFTER
I'VE HAD LUNCH AND A FEW MEXICAN BEERS
NEVER SAW THE TWO PGA STARS
FOR ONCE I HAD THE EXPERIENCE
IN MY CAMERA IT WAS NOT FANTASY
THE TAXI WAS A SPEED TRIP
BACK TO CLUB MED WE FLEW

CHECKED THE POOL LAURA WAS NOT THERE
UP TO THE ROOM I WENT OPENED THE DOOR
LAURA WAS NUDE LYING ON THE BED
GET SOME CLOTHES ON MEET ME AT THE BAR
OVER PINA COLADAS MY STOREY UNFOLDED
ALL IMAGES WERE CLEAR AS A BELL
TURN THE TAPE RECORDER ON
AND HERE IS HOW IT WENT
AFTER THE FULL STOREY MISSING NO DETAILS
WE ORDERED TWO MORE PINO COLADAS
ALL SHE SAID ANOTHER CHAPTER FOR MY BOOK

OUR WEEK WAS GOING TO END
AFTER WE DISCUSSED THE COLLEGE OF MEXICO
THE STRUCTURE WAS SIMPLE STATES
RULED BY THE FEDARALS IN MEXICO CITY
LANCE SHE LOOKED AT ME
LETS GO TO THE ISLA MUJERES
MEANS ISLAND OF THE WOMEN
I HAVE BOOKED US THERE
VAMENOS IN MY BEST MEXICAN LINGO

A THOUSAND YEARS

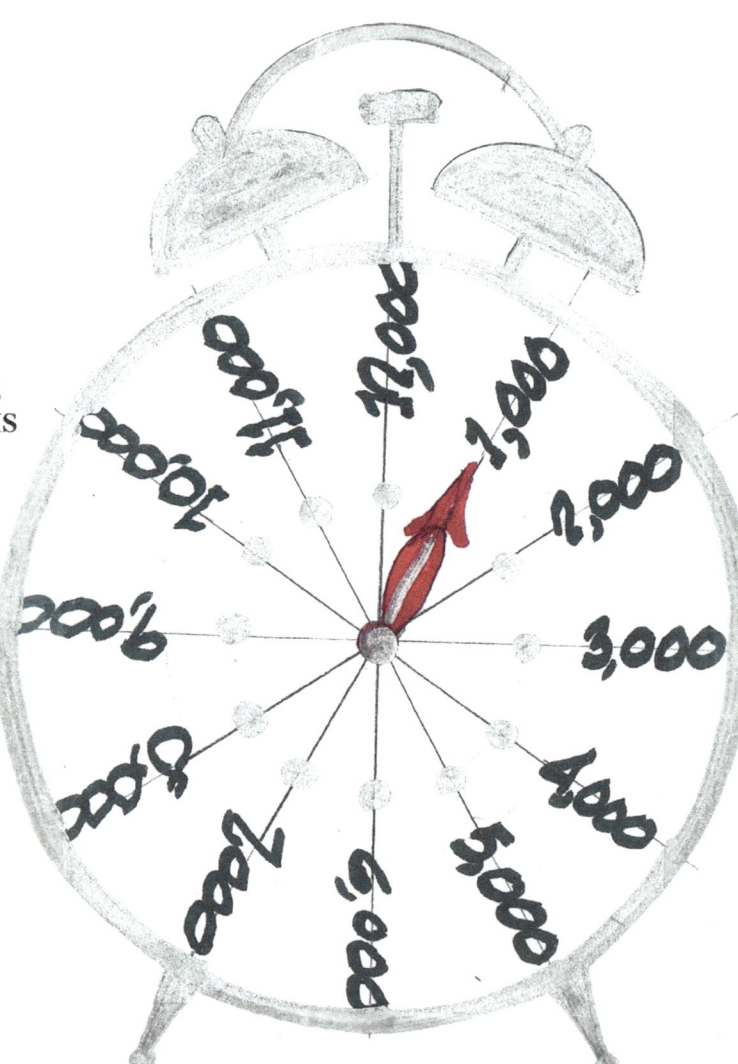

I HAVE LIVED
A THOUSAND YEARS
SHED AN OCEAN BLUE
OF WARM WET TEARS
WHITE CAPS SPARKLE
SURPRISES BRING JOY
LOVE AN HEART FELT
HAPPYNESS FOR ALL TO SEE
THE INBETWEEN TROUGHS
FORMED BY CURRENTS
WITH WAYWORD WINDS
SEEMS LIKE THE LOW
CYCLE OF HURT WITHIN
DEPRESSION AND DEATH
TIME WILL FIX IT FOR
UP TO WHITE CAPS
YOU WILL GO
IMORTALITY ONLY A FEW
WILL NEVER KNOW
ACTORS, AUTHORS
AND POETS TOO

ARCHITECTS, ENGINEERS
HAVE ENHANCED THE
HUMAN EXPERIENCE
WITH THEIR WORK A GLOW
NO ONE REALLY CARES
FOR ALL FUTURE GENERATIONS
IT'S THE HIGH TECH WORLD
KINDERGARDEN TO PHD
THE FUTURE UNKOWN
THE SEEDS HAVE BE PLANTED
THE WATERING HAS TO FOLLOW
BUT WHO HAS THE CAN
WE WILL NEVER KNOW
RE-BOOT YOUR LIFE
LOOK AT TIME OF YOUR BEING
FOR YOU HAVE TOO
LIVED
A THOUSAND YEARS

THEODORO CORONA LUNA
JULY 29, 2018

THE PATH

LIFE'S JOURNEY

MAY YOUR PATH BE KIND
NOT TO NARROW NOT TO WIDE
GENTLE UPS AND DOWNS
PLACES TO REST AND CONTEMPT
THE JOY OF LIVING AND THE PATH OF
YOUR CHOICE FOR THE BEST ONE TO TAKE

PUT ALL YOUR BURDEN'S IN
YOUR BACKPACK FOR THEY WILL
SOON DISAPPEAR FOR YOU
AND YOUR LOVE ONE AND FAITHFUL
COMPANION WILL PROTECT YOU
FROM THE CREATURES OF THE NIGHT
UNLESS IT'S AN EARTHQUAKE

ALL OF YOUR LIFE'S HURTS
DIMINISH WITH THE WONDERFUL
WHISPER OF THE MAGIC WILDERNESS
NO MATTER WHAT THE PROFESSONELS
IN TUNE WITH THE WILDERNESS
IS NOT OFTEN THEIR ADVICE

TAKE AS LONG AS YOU CAN BEING
ONE WITH NATURES'S BEST MEDICINE
OR AS LONG AS THE FOOD LASTS
THE CRYSTAL-CLEAR LAKE IS NOW IN SIGHT
THE PLACE TO PITCH YOUR TENT
AND GATHER WOOD FOR A FIRE

AT TWILIGHT THE TROUT STARTED
JUMPING FOR DINNER BEFORE BED
THE STARS ARE MAKING THEIR PRESENT
TIME TO UNROLL YOUR BEDROLLS
HAVE A NIGHT-CAP AND CODDLE
THE WHISPER AND HEALING STARTS

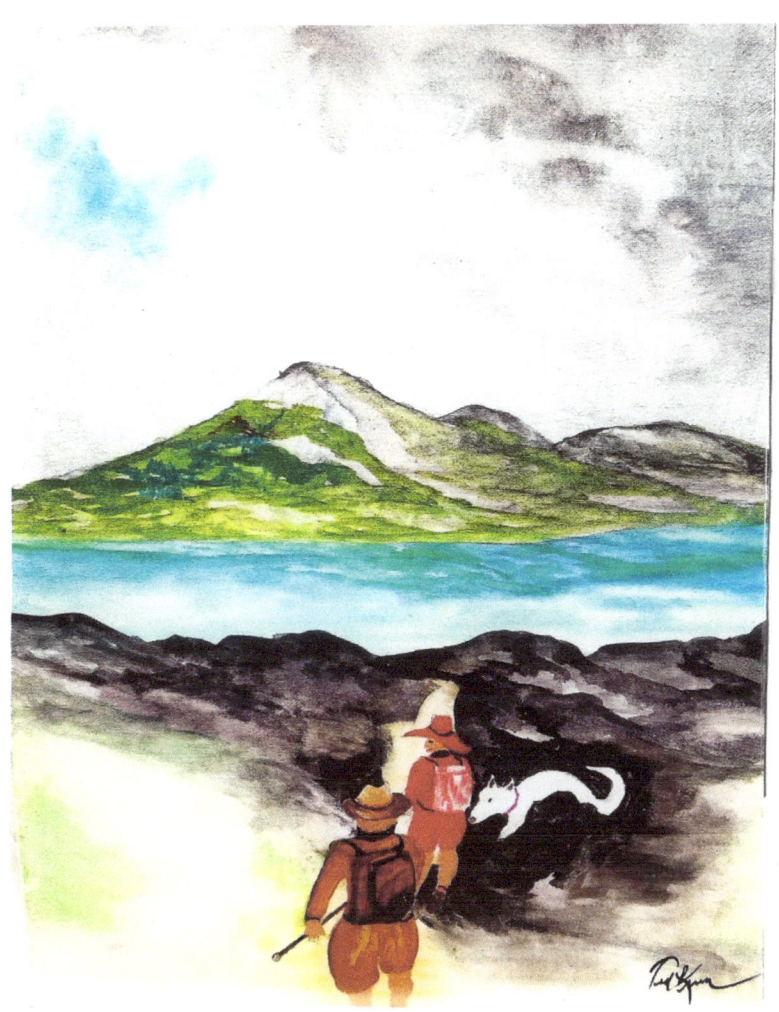

YOU AND YOUR LOVE AFTER A FEW DAYS
HAVE A MILD HIGH-COUNTRY SUNBURN
IT WAS TIME TO GO BACK DOWN THE PATH
TO WHERE YOU PARKED THE CAR
WITH CLEAR THROUGHTS AND
RESOLVE FOR YOUR LIFE'S PATH
THE WILDERNESS HEALING WON

CONGRADULATIONS
MOMMY

ACCORDING TO THE ACADEMY
ACCOUNTANTS "pooch and pussy cat"
YOU ARE THE ONLY WINNER
FOR THE DOGGIE AND GATO
ACADEMY AWARDS 2019
FOR BEST PERFORMANCE
BY MOMMIES FOR THIS YEAR
THE HEINZ 57 OSCAR
WILL BE PRESENTED TO
YOU AT DINNER TIME

YOUR VOTE SCORE WAS
THE HIGHEST IN ALL
OF THE CATEGORIES
LOVE, KINDNESS, HEALTH
COMPANIONSHIP, CARING
MOST OF ALL FUN
THE HIGHEST SCORE
WAS FOR
DOGGIE AND GATO TREATS

THE ACADEMY AND WE
REQUEST YOU MAINTAIN
ALL OF THE ABOVE
TILL NEXT YEAR AWARDS
FOR THE YEAR 2020
I ASKED DAD'S TO FORGE
MY SIGNITURE

WITH ETERNAL DOGGIE
LOVE

DESTING

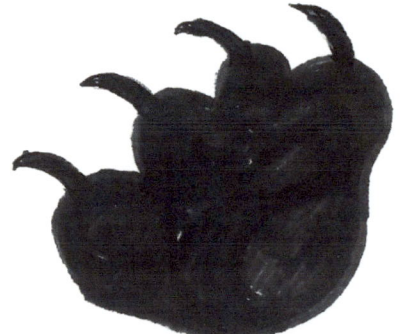

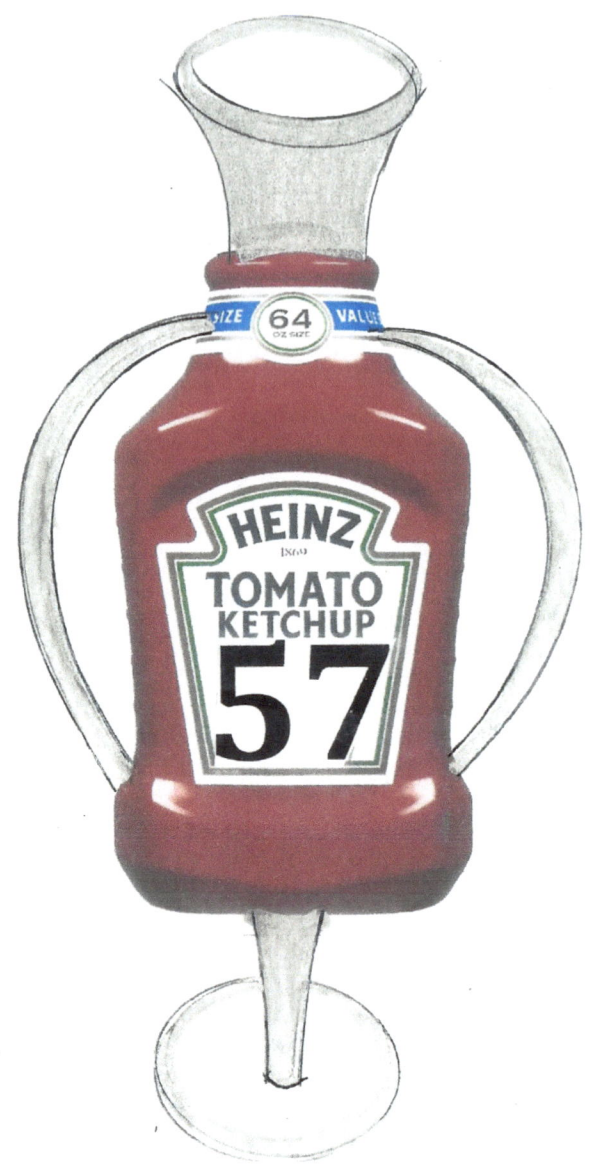

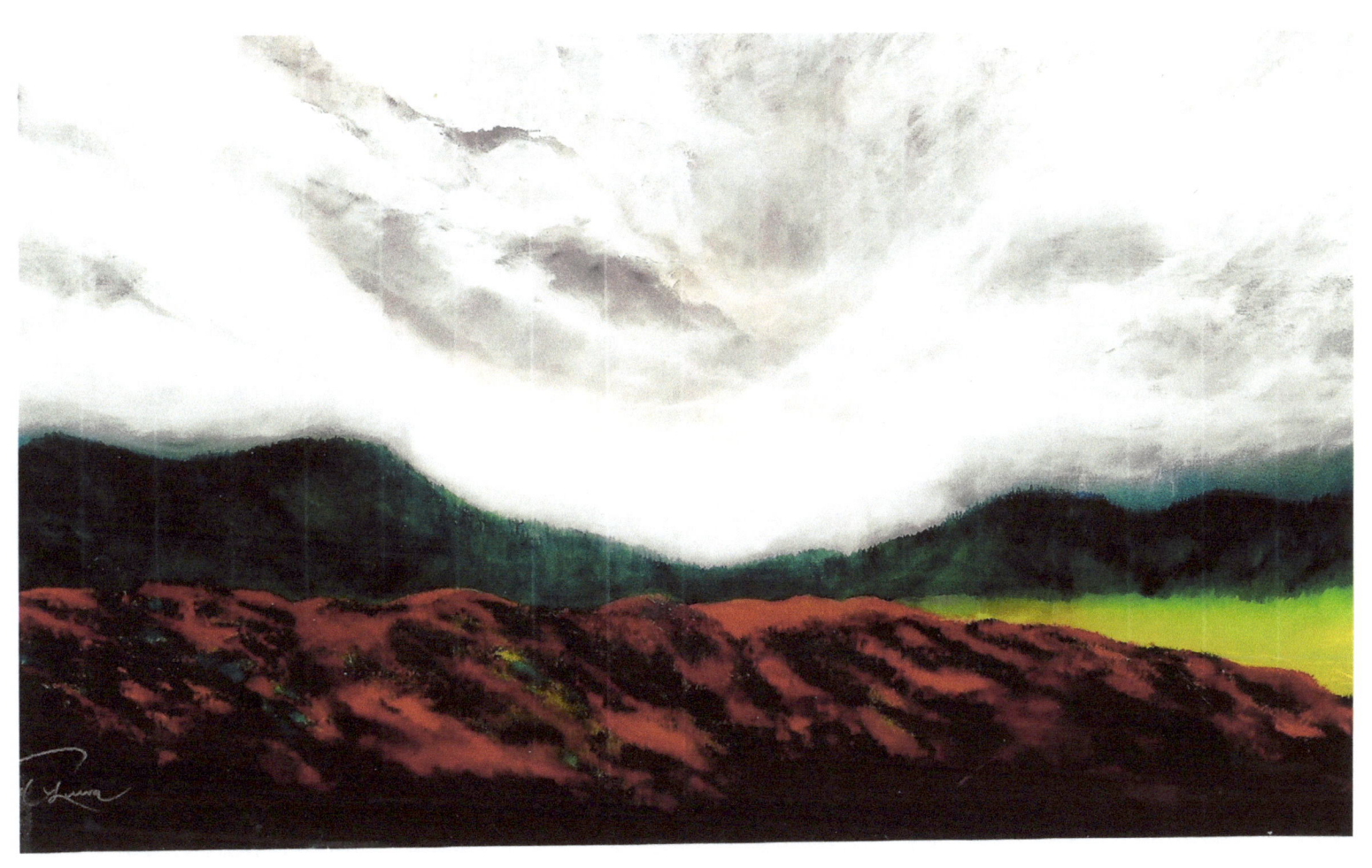

SCRUB OAK IN LATE FALL COLOR
FIRST WINTER SNOW STORM
BREWING

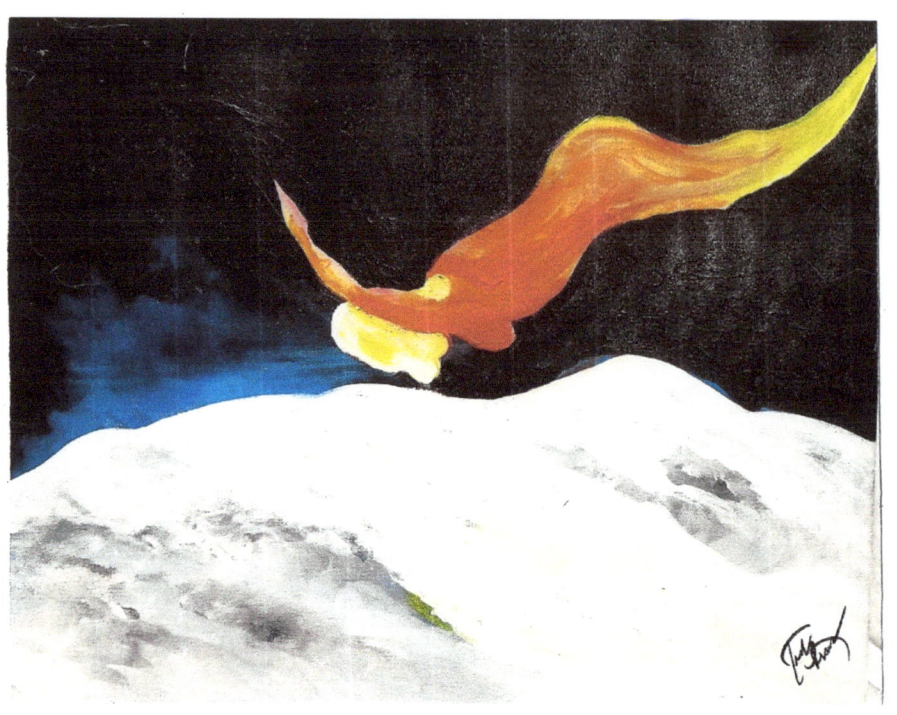

FEARS

BEING ALONE UNTIL I LEARNED TO LIKE MYSELF **PEOPLES OPINIONS** THEY WOULD HAVE OPINIONS ANYWAY **FAILURE** JUST STEPPING STONES TO SUCCESS **REJECTION** HAVE FAITH IN YOUR SELF	**HATE** NOTHING MORE THAN IGNORANCE **LOVE** NO OTHER PERSON NEEDS TO LOVE BACK **RIDICULE** LAUGH AT MYSELF **SUCCESS** OK TO BE THE BEST I CAN DO	**CHANGE** METAMORPHOSIS OF LIFE **RELIGION** CHOOSE ONE IF ANY **LIFE MATE** SHE WILL ALWAYS CHOOSE **FUN** ANYTHING THAT MAKES YOU GLAD YOUR ALIVE
PAIN ITS NECESSARY FOR GROWTH **TRUTH** SEE THE UGLINESS OF LIES **LIFE** IT DEPENDS SOLELY ON ATTITUDE **DEATH** ONLY A BEGINNING	**GROWING OLD** BEAUTY OF DAILY WISDOM **DARK** SEEING THE STARS AT NIGHT **PAST** HURT ONLY IF I ALLOW **FUTURE** MOMENT ALL THAT MATTERS	AUTHOR UNKNOWN I INCLUDE THIS BECAUSE I LIKED IT FOR A REALITY CHECK THEODORO CORONA LUNA

LANCE & LAURA
ISLA MUJERES

THE CLUB MED VAN TOOK US
TO PORTO JUAREZ TO TAKE THE FERRY
FOR THE 30 MINUTE RIDE TO THE ISLA
IT WAS FULLY PACTED WITH TOURIST
THE BOAT WAS POWERED BY
DIESEL FUEL AND WE SMELLED IT

ARRIVING AT THE WOODEN DOCK
EL CAPITAN SHOUTED
LA ISLA LA ISLA LA ISLA
LAURA SMILED LOOK LANCE
THERE'S THE TAXI STAND
WHAT! GOLF CARTS WITH
REAR SEATING NO CLUBS

THE SLOW RIDE TO THE HOTEL
WAS THROUGH THE MARKET PLACE
WHAT A BEAUTIFUL SITES
LAURA WE ARE BACK 100 YEARS
IN THE HISTORY OF THE COLLEGE
OF MEXICO

THE NEW HOTEL ON THE BEACH
REPLACED THE PREVIOUS ONE
THAT WAS LEVELED BY A HURRICANE
SO OUR DRIVER WAS A HISTORIAN
OR JUST WANTING A BIG TIP
GLASSES OF CHAMPAGNE GREATED US

LAURA LET ME CARRY YOU
ACROSS THE THRESHOLD
AS I OPENED THE DOOR
TO THE TOP FLOOR SUITE
EVERY CREATURE COMFORT
WAS THERE A FEW I NEVER KNEW

UNPACKING TOOK A FEW MINUTES
WE ARE WELL RESTED LET'S
GO EXPLORE WE CAN WALK
AND SEE MOST OF THE ISLA
WITH CAMERA AND NOTE BOOK
VAMINOUS LINDA
IN MY LEARNED MEXICAN BROWG

IT SOON BECAME APPARENT
MOST OF ISLA'S POPULATION
SPOKE ENGLISH BETTER THAN US
THE ISLA WAS MAGIC AND
EVERY ONE WAS FRIENDLY
BEST FOOD AND DRINK CHEAP

COLORS AND MUSIC EVERY WHERE
GREETED LAURA AND ME IN DELIGHT
SUNSET ORANGE FIRE- BALL
SINKING INTO THE SEA
I TOOK THE BEST IMAGES EVER
ON EASTER MORNING WE WENT
DEEP SEA FISHING

ONLY KEEPING FOUR YELLOW TAIL
TUNA AND NEVER WANTING MORE
OUR SMALL BOAT CAPTAIN
WOULD TAKE ONE TUNA
TO A RESTURANT HE KNEW
AND THEY WOULD PREPARE IT FOR US

I ASKED HIM ABOUT THE OTHER THREE
HE SMILED AND SAID THEY ARE FOR ME
IT WAS MID-AFTERNOON
SITTING UNDER A TREE THAT BEGAN
OUR FEAST MARGARITA'S AND MORE
I ASKED LAURA TO CALL A TAXI
DIDN'T NEED TO THERE WAS ONE
AT THE FRONT DOOR

LOCAL KNOWLEDGE WAS JUST TO ASK
ON THE FOLLOWING NIGHT SITTING
AFTER DINNER AT THE BAR
A YOUNG COUPLE WERE LAUGHING
WE OVERHEARD THEM TALKING
ABOUT THEIR DAY TRIP TO CONTOY

NEXT MORNING, WE HAD DETAILS
LAURA MADE RESERVATIONS
FOR OUR ADVENTURE TO
THE SMALL ISLA CONTOY
WE HAD TO BE AT THE DOCK
NO LATER THAN EIGHT

WE BOTH HAD LONG SLEEVE WHITE
COTTON SHIRTS AND PANTS TO MATCH
SWIM SUITS INSTEAD OF BRIEFS
SWIM FINS AND SNORKEL MASKS
TO BE PROVIDED WITH FOOD AND DRINK
EL CAPITAN AND MATE COULD NOT DATE

THE SEA WORTHY BOAT COULD
ONLY TAKE TWELVE WITH
LAURA AND ME IT MADE IT FULL
UNDER A SHADE SAIL OFF WE WENT
ALL OF THE OTHERS WERE YOUNG
KNOWING ONLY TO HAVE FUN

OUT OF PORT JUST A FEW MILES
TWO BEAUTIFUL YOUNG LADIES
STRIPPED TO BIRTHDAY SUITS
NO ONE ELSE DID BUT ALL
ENJOYED THE SIGHT
EL CAPITAN AND MATE IGNORED
THE SIGHT THEY SEEN ALOT MORE

THE SEA WAS MIRROR FLAT
EL CAPITAN STOPPED THE BOAT
WE ARE HALF THERE AND
BELOW THERE IS A WONDERFUL
REEF TO EXPLORE GET READY
TO SWIM BUT NO ONE MOVED

I WATCHED THE MATE JUMP
INTO THE SEA CAME UP
WITH A LOBSTER, HELD IN HIS HAND
IT HAD NO CLAWS I KNEW THEN
THAT THE REEF WAS SAFE
I WAS THE FIRST ONE INTO THE SEA

ALL OF THE OTHERS FOLLOWED
NO LONGER AFRAID SHOUTS OF JOY
MY WATER-PROOF CAMERA
ALWAYS WITH ME THEN I SAW
LAURA SMILING THROUGH HER MASK
SHE THREW ME A WATER KISS

BEFORE I WOULD EXPLORE
THIS WONDERFUL REEF WORLD
LOOKED AROUND AND WOW
THE NAKED LADIES FLOATING
ON CRISTAL CLEAR WATER
LIKE MERMAIDS OF THE SEA

THE REEF CORAL AND FISH
WAS LIKE NOTHING I HAD EVER SEEN
IT WAS AN UNDERWATER MOUNTAIN
SIX TO TWENTY FEET DEEP
TAKING IMAGES LIKE NEVER BEFORE
THE GROUP SCATERED ON THEIR OWN

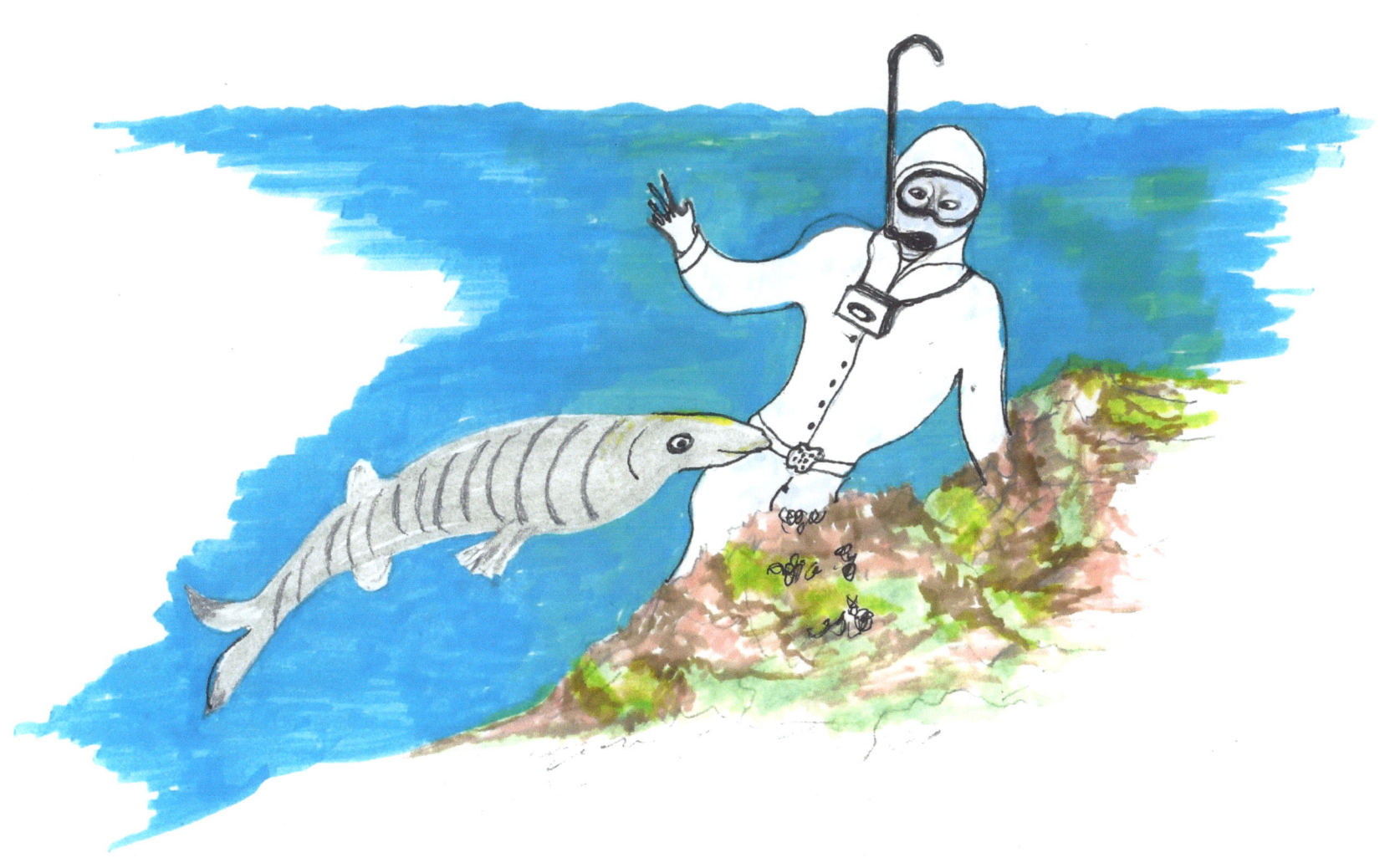

WHEN I TURNED AROUND AND LOOKED
I WAS ASTOUNDED A FISH SMILING
TELEPATHIC COMMUNICATION
THE SEVEN FOOT BARRACUDA
LONG NOSE AND RAZOR TEETH
SCALES MUTICULORED DANCING

DON'T BE AFRAID SHE SAID
I WOUNT HURT YOU
FLOAT ON THE SURFACE
AND LOOK DOWN ON ME
THAT WAY WE CAN TALK
FOR TALES I CAN TELL

YOU CAN CALL ME BARRA
AND YOUR NAME, LANCE HE SAID
I LIVE A GREAT LIFE HERE IN THE SEA
WONDERFUL FOOD TO EAT
SWIMMING AROUND AS YOU SEE
WHEN MY TIME COMES, I LAY MY EGGS

I NEVER KNOW WHO THE FATHER TO BE
I NEVER RAISE MY CHILDREN
THEY ON THEIR OWN
AS THEY GROW SWIMMING ALONE
I OFTEN WONDER IF IT WAS ME
FATHERS ARE BACHAELORS ALWAYS ALONE

LANCE ASK BARRA TO COME CLOSER
SO, I CAN GET AN IMAGE OF YOU AND ME
HE TOOK MANY AND THEN
THE BOAT HORN SOUNDED FOR
THE GROUP TO RETURN
SAYING HEARTFELT GOODBYE TO BARRA
BACK ON THE BOAT AND DRYING OUT
EL CAPITAN IN HIS MEXICAN SHOUT
TO CONTOY NEXT STOP FOR LUNCH
WE WADED THE WATER
TO A CRISTAL WHITE BEACH
TREES AND THEY STARTED A FIRE

WE SOON FOUND OUT WHY THE FIRE
THE MATE HAD GATHERED LOBSTERS
FOR OUR MAGNIFICENT FEAST
MEX VEGIES, BEER, JOSE CURVO
SHORT REST, BACK TO THE BOAT
NON-STOP BACK TO THE MUJERES

WE WOULD TALK BACK AT THE HOTEL
THE TWO YOUNG LADIES BODYS
WERE RED TO MATCH THE LOBSTERS
THEY SET ON THE DECK SHIVERING
WE WRAPED THEM WITH COLD TOWELS
AND GAVE THEM GOOD CHILED WATER
THEIR LARK TURN INTO A BARK
LAURA AND I THANK EACH OTHER
THE FULL COTTON BODY SUIT WORKED

EVERY ONE TIPPED EL CAPITAN AND MATE
THEY HELPED US OFF THE BOAT
EL CAPITAN SOFTLY SAID TO EVERYONE
ADIOS AMIGOS, WE WALKED TO THE HOTEL
TIRED BUT ENERGISED TO DINNER WE WENT
LATER WE WOULD SHARE THE DAY

LANCE, LAURA ASKED AFTER WE SHARED
IMAGES, HER NOTES AND STORIES
HOW IN THE WORLD DID YOU GET?
YOUR TELEPATHIC POWERS
IT MUST HAVE BEEN
DUE TO SIR LANCELOT GENES

DROP IN BED NO PAJAMAS REQUIRED
LAURA ASKED LANCE TIME TO LEAVE
WHERE ARE WE GOING NEXT
LANCE ANSWERED I REALLY DON'T KNOW
IT'S WHERE TED WILL SEND US NEXT

LANCE & LAURA

CHICHEN ITZA

EARLY MORNING, THEY LEFT
THE HOTEL TO THE FERRY DOCK
THE FERRY WAS THE SAME ONE
WITH THE SAME SMELLS
AND CAPITAN WITH LESS
TOURESTS AND LOCALS

THEY CHATTED ABOUT THE
GREAT TIME THEY HAD ON
THE ISLA AND CONTOY
EVERY THING WAS DOWNLOADED
IN THE LAP TOPS NOT EDITED
ARRIVEING AT PORTO JUAREZ

ADIOS EL CAPITAN
LOOK LANCE A REAL TAXI
SENIOR ONDE VAMANIOUS
LAURA SMILED SAID TO
RENT A CARO POR FAVORED
THE CABBIE SAID SI

IN BROKEN ENGLISH
HE SAID AVIS OR HERTZ
IN CANCUN AVIS GIVES ME
KICK BACK PER PERSONA
THIS IS THE MEXICAN WAY
VAMANIUOUS

WE TIPPED HIM WELL
THE OFFICE WAS VERY COOL
BUENOS DIAS THE LADY SAID
LANCE STATED THEY NEEDED
A CAR, LAURA ONLY WITH
THE BEST POSSIBLE A/C

WITH PAPER ROAD MAP
AND HEFTY MEXICAN INSURANCE
IT WAS EASY TO LEAVE CANCUN
NOT TO FAR TO CHICHEN ITZA
WHEN THE ENCOUNTERED THE
FIRST TOPES THAT BOUNCED THE CAR

LANCE LOOKED AT LAURA
I KNOW NOW WHAT THE SIGN
MENT I THOUGHT IT WAS
A VILLAGE BUT LOOK
THE YUCATAN HUTS SCATTERED
BEAUTIFUL AND SIMPLE

THEY ONLY NEEDED PROTECTION
FROM THE RAIN AND HAVE SHADE
WOW SEE THE TV ANTENNAS
EACH HAD A BLACK AND WHITE
POSTAGE STAMP TV WITH
THE ELDERS GLUED FOR THE
THE MEXICAN SOAPBOX SERIES

HOWEVER, THE CHILDREN
WERE PLAYING OUT-DOORS
ON THE ROAD WE ENCOUNTED
MORE AND MORE TOPES
LANCE SAID WHAT WAS ONLY
TWO HOURS ON THE ROAD

PER THE STATED MILEAGE
ON THE MAP HAS TURNED
INTO A FOUR-HOUR DRIVE
LET'S STOP IN VALLADALID
FOR LUNCH AND REST
GREAT IDEA LUARA

LANCE NO STREET FOOD CARTS
LOOK A NICE HOTEL
FOOD SHOULD BE SAFE
LAURA ORDERED FISH WITH VEGS
LANCE ORDERED A SHRIMP SALAD
CORONAS ALL AROUND

BACK IN CAR LANCE
LOOKED AT THE MAP
DEPENDING ON THE TOPES
WE HAVE LESS THAN AN HOUR
TO CHICHEN ITZA THEY
HAVE A HOTEL ON SITE

LANCE DID YOU MAKE RESERVATIONS
NO LAURA I THOUGHT YOU DID
THE LUCK OF THE DRAW
LET'S HOPE IT WILL WORK
THE ROAD POLIZA ARE IN A
JEEP WITH FOUR MEN
WITH ASSAULT RIFES

THEY SEEM TO KEEP THE PEACE
THROUGH INTIMIDATION
WE ARRIVED PARKED THE CAR
WALKED TO THE COOL CHECK-IN
DESK WITH ONE NICE WOMEN
AND A TALL MAN BEHIND HER

WE ASKED HER FOR A ROOM
SHE LOOKED AT US WITH A SAD FACE
SENIOR WE ARE FULLY BOOKED
NO ROOMS AVAILABLE FOR A WEEK
THE TALL HANDSOME MAN
STEPPED FORWARD TOOK
LANCE'S HAND I WILL OFFER

MY APARTMENT THAT OVERLOOKS
THE DINING ROOM AND I WILL
GO AND STAY WITH MY GIRL
FOR AS LONG AS YOU LIKE
THE CHARGES WILL BE NORMAL
LAURA ALMOST FAINTED

THE APARTMENT HAD THE MAYAN
FLAVOR WITH FULL INFORMATION
ABOUT THE MAYAN HISTORY
AND THIS HISTORIC SITE WITH
SUGGESTIONS ABOUT VISTITATION
ONE WAS TO START BEFORE SUNRISE
WHEN IT WAS COOL

LANCE LET'S GO HAVE DINNER
THEY WERE ESCORDED TO A NICE
TABLE LAURA NOTICE LANCE
GREY AND FEELING SICK
THE WAITER SAW THIS AND
RETURNED WITH A CUP OF TEA

SENIOR PLEASE GO TO YOUR ROOM
AND DRINK THIS TEA, PLEASE GO
LAURA SAID I'LL WAIT FOR YOU
LANCE DID AS INSTUCTED
HE TOOK THE TEA DRINK AND
JUST A FEW MINUTES LATER

RACED TO THE BATH ROOM
IT ALL CAME OUT TOP AND BOTTOM
WHEN HE WAS DONE, HE
FELT GOOD AND BACK TO NORMAL
WENT BACK TO THE DINING ROOM
ASKED THE WAITER TWO QUESTIONS

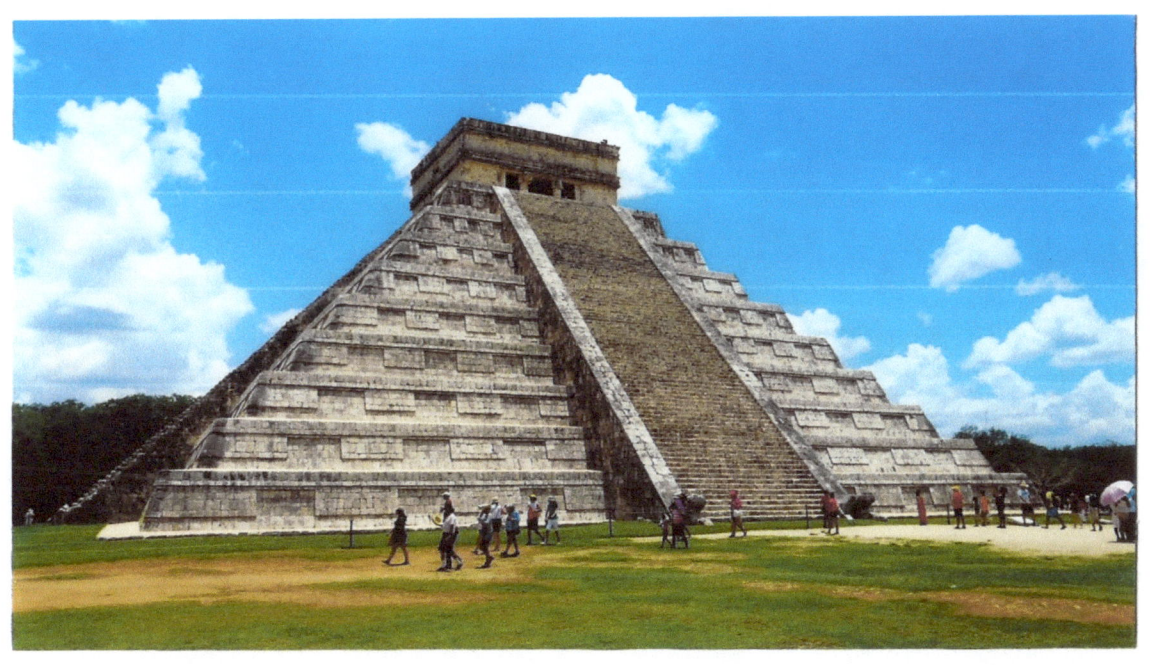

THE KIND WAITER TOLD LANCE
THAT HE HAD EXPERIENCED
MONTEZUMAS REVENGE
THE UNWASHED LETTUCE IN
THE LUNCH HE HAD EATEN
THE TEA WAS MONZANIA TEA
LAURA SAID WE WILL BUY
A CARTON
UP BEFORE SUNRISE WITH
A LIGHT BREAKFAST OUT TO THE
SITE THEY WENT FOR A NEW
ADVENTURE CAMERA AND RECORDER
SUN HATS AND STP 50
THEY WOULD START AT
EL CASTILLO WITH GUIDE BOOK

THE FOOD FOR DINER WAS THE
BEST MEAL EVER OF COURSE
LANCE HANDED THE WAITER
A HANDFUL OF DOLLARS
AND SINCERE THANKS
UP TO BED THEY WENT

BOTH OF THEM COULD ONLY
MARVEL ABOUT THE COLLEGE
OF THE VAST MAYAN EMPIRE
AND IT'S ONGOING DISCOVERIES
WHEN THEY ENTERED THE
EL CASTILLO AND GAZED AT

THE GOLD LEPPARD LANCE
REMEMISED ABOUT THE ONE
IN AFRICA BUT NOTHING HAPPENED
SO MUCH TO SEE EVEN FOR A WEEK
THEY COULD ONLY MARVEL
AT THE VAST OPEN SPACES
OF IT'S LAND PLANNING DESIGN

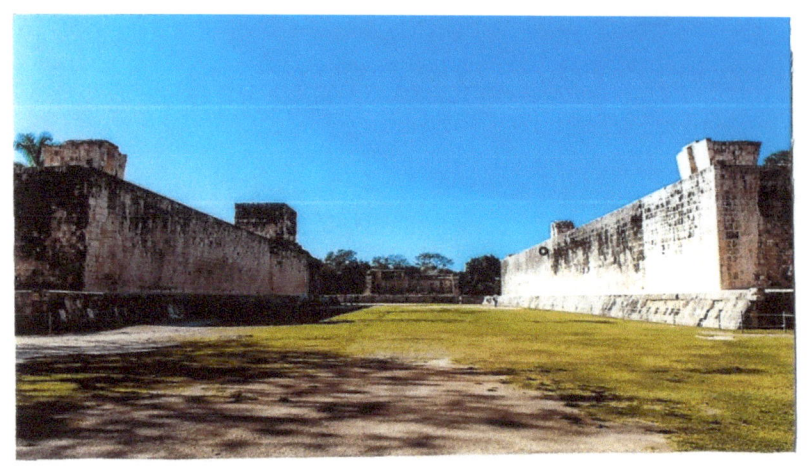

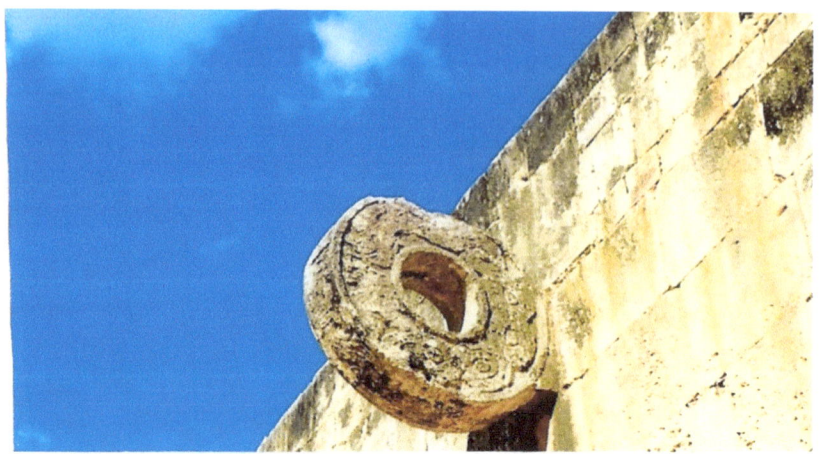

NEXT TO THE BALL COURT
LANCE KNEW THAT THERE WERE
MANY HUNDREDS THROUGHT OUT
THE VAST MAYAN EMPIRE
BUT THIS ONE WAS THE SUPER BOWL
ONLY THE BEST OF THE BEST
WOULD PLAY HERE

TALL STONE WALLS OPEN WITH
A SMALL TEMPLE AT EACH END
SMALL HIGH UP STONE ROCK
ON THE TWO WALLS
WITH A SMALL HOLE IN THE
MIDDLE AT CENTER OF THE COURT

THE GAME WAS SIMPLE AND
RULES WERE SET BY THE ELITE
COUNCIL THAT WATCHED EVERY
MOVE THAT EACH TEAM
MADE EACH TEAM HAD ONLY
TWO MEN NOT OFTEN THREE

THE FULL BODY CONTACT WITH OUT
THE USE OF HANDS MADE KEEPING
THE SMALL RUBBER BALL AIRBORNE
AND PASS IT THRUGH THE HOLE
BECAME THE ONLY GOAL
FIRST TEAM TO SCORE
ENDED THE GAME

THE COUNCIL WOULD DECIDE
THE FATE OF THE WINNERS AND
LOOSERS IT OFTEN DEPENDED
ON HOW GOOD THE GAME WAS
OR HOW MUCH THEY HAD TO DRINK
OR THE POINTS GIVEN WHEN
THE BALL TOUCHED THE GROUND

LAURA WAS BUSY RECORDING
AND TALKING TO THE GUIDE
LANCE DECIDED TO WALK THE
FULL LENGTH OF THE BALL COURT
TO THE SMALL END CHAPEL
HE TOOK MANY IMAGES

THE GATE TO THE CHAPEL
WAS OPEN SO HE STEPPED INSIDE
SMALL AND BEAUTIFUL
STONE WORK ARCHED CEILINGS
HE SAT TO REST WHEN
HE SAW AND EMERGING IMAGE

IT MATERIZED WITH A SMILE
STANDING IN FRONT OF HIM
WAS AN ANCIENT MAYAN
FIVE FEET TALL, BLACK LONG HAIR
AND EYES, CLAD ONLY WITH
A LOIN CLOTH AND LARGE
CERIMONIAL HEAD CROWN
HELD IN PLACE WITH A CHIN STRAP

THE TELLIPATHIC COMMUNICATIONS
BEGAN HE SAID MY NAME IS
TAAVI NAMED AFTER THE ADORNED
AND YOURS, LANCE SAID
AFTER SIR LANCELOT A KNIGHT
I HAVE WAITED MANY CENTURIES
TO TALK TO SOMEONE MY SPIRIT
WILL NEVER LEAVE THE TEMPLE
MY FAMILY WERE ONE OF THE ELITE
WHEN I COULD WALK, THEY
GAVE ME A RUBBER BALL
SOON TO FOLLOW WITH MENTORS
THEY TAUGHT ME THE BALL COURT
VERY SOON I WAS PLAYING
IN LESSER COURTS IN THE EMPIRE

LANCE THOUGHT TO HIMSELF
THE MINOR LEAGUES STEPPING STONE
TO THE MAJORS AT THE SUPERBOWL
MY FAMILY CAME TO CHICHEN ITZA
FOR MY FIRST AND ONLY GAME
I SCORED THE ONE AND ONLY GOAL

THE COUNCIL PROCLAIMED
ALL PLAYERS WOULD LOSE THEIR
HEADS BECAUSE IT WAS A GREAT GAME
IT WAS FAST BEING THE LAST ONE
I SAW THE HEADS SET ON SPIKES
THEN IT WAS MY TURN AND
MY SPIRIT WENT TO THIS TEMPLE

LANCE ASKED TAAVI TO TAKE
HIS IMAGE WITH ONE OF HIM
TOGETHER TAAVI AGREED
TAAVI THEN FADED INTO THE SHADOWS
LANCE WAS AGAIN ALL ALONE
HE COULD NOT WAIT TO TELL
LAURA AND SEE THE IMAGES

IT WAS GETTING HOT
HE FOUND LAURA AND WENT
BACK TO THE HOTEL TO REST
HE TOLD HER THE STORY
WHICH SHE RECORDED
HE PLAYED BACK THE IMAGES
ON HIS CAMERA, TAAVI WAS NOT
THERE ONLY LANCE AND THE TEMPLE
SPIRITS CAN'T BE PHOTOGRAPH
HE WAS DISAPPOINTED

THEY SPENT A FEW MORE DAYS
AND OTHER SUROUNDING AREAS
THEY ENJOYED THE MAYAN
EMPIRE AND WHAT WAS LEFT OF IT
BACK AT THE HOTEL IT
WAS TIME TO LEAVE

LAURA WANTED TO SEE
THE FRENCH INSPIRED CITY
NORTH CALLED MERIDA
JUST A FEW HOURS AWAY
DEPENDING ON THE TOPES
THEY ARRIVED EARLY AFTERNOON

DRIVING THROUGH MAGNIFICENT
BOULEVARD'S AND MAJESTIC
BUILDINGS THEY CHECKED INTO
A FINE-LOOKING FRENCH HOTEL
LAURA STATED THAT THE
FRENCH AND ENGLISH INFLUENCE

SEEMED TO BE INMOST EVERY
COLLEGE IN THE UNIVERSITY
I THOUGHT I WAS IN EUROPE
AFTER A FINE DINNER FRENCH
STYLE, THEY CLIMBED IN BED

SEEING THE CITY FOR A FEW
MORE DAYS TAKING MANY
IMAGES AND LOTS OF RECORDINGS
LANCE, THEY HAVE AN AIRPORT
WHERE TO NEXT LANCE SAID
I DON'T KNOW EVER
TED SENDS US

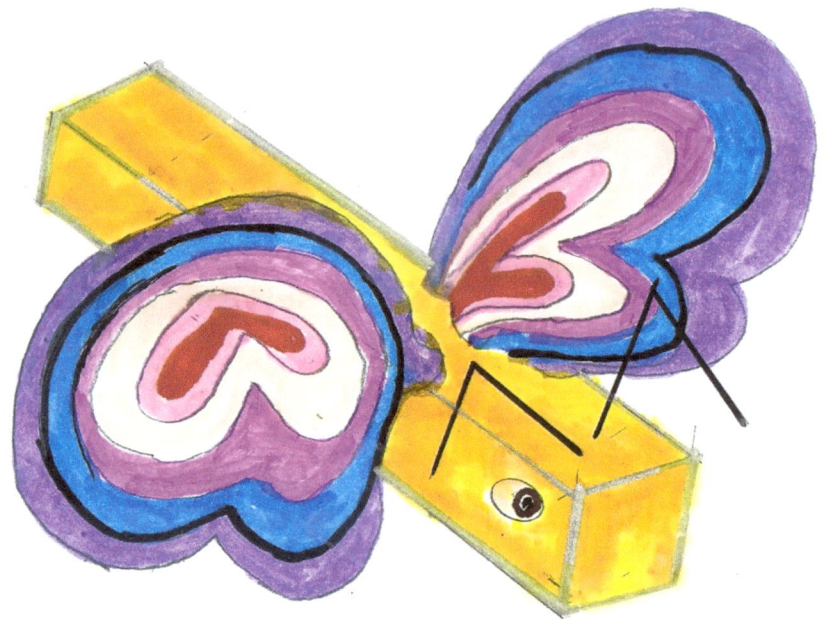

BUTTERFLIES
WHY ARE THEY CALLED

MONARCKS GATHER DARKEN THE SKY
FROM THE NORTH TO THE SOUTH THEY FLY
TO A SPECIAL PLACE IN MEXICO
THE MEXICANS CELEBRATE
MOSTLY IN TREES SOME ON THE GROUND
THEY WILL RETURN SOUTH TO NORTH
HOW DO THEY KNOW
WHEN THE TIME IS RIGHT TO RETURN

IN OUR CULTURE PAST AND PRESENT
THEY ARE CALLED MANY NAMES
RUSSIA "BABOCHKA" LITTLE SOUL
FRANCE "PAPILLON" SIOUX INDIANS
"FLUTTERING WINGS"
ENGLISH COLONIES BROUGHT THEM WEST
BELIEVED THAT WITCHES TURNED INTO
WINGED CREATURES AND STOLED BUTTER
NOW YOU KNOW WHY THEY ARE CALLED
BUTTERFLIES

THEODORO CORONA LUNA

JOY TO THE EYE WHEN THEY FLY
OFTEN JUST A FEW DASHING AROUND
FLUTTERING WINGS REFLECTS THE SUNLIGHT
WHITE, YELLOW ALL COLORS BEYOND
THE RAINBOW MULTI PATTERNS
THAT ONLY AN ARTIST COULD PAINT

\FOUR TO FIVE MILLION YEARS OLD
A SCIENTIST TOLD, HARD TO BELIEVE
THAT'S VERY OLD FOR THE MOTH
FAMILY THAT HAS FOUR STAGES
THEY HAVE EVOLVED AS ROYALTY
WE ARE BLESSED
IN SEEING THEM TODAY

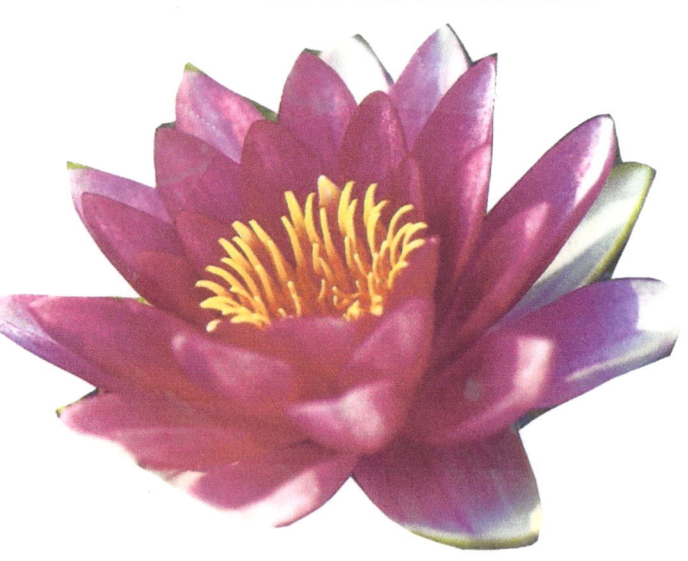

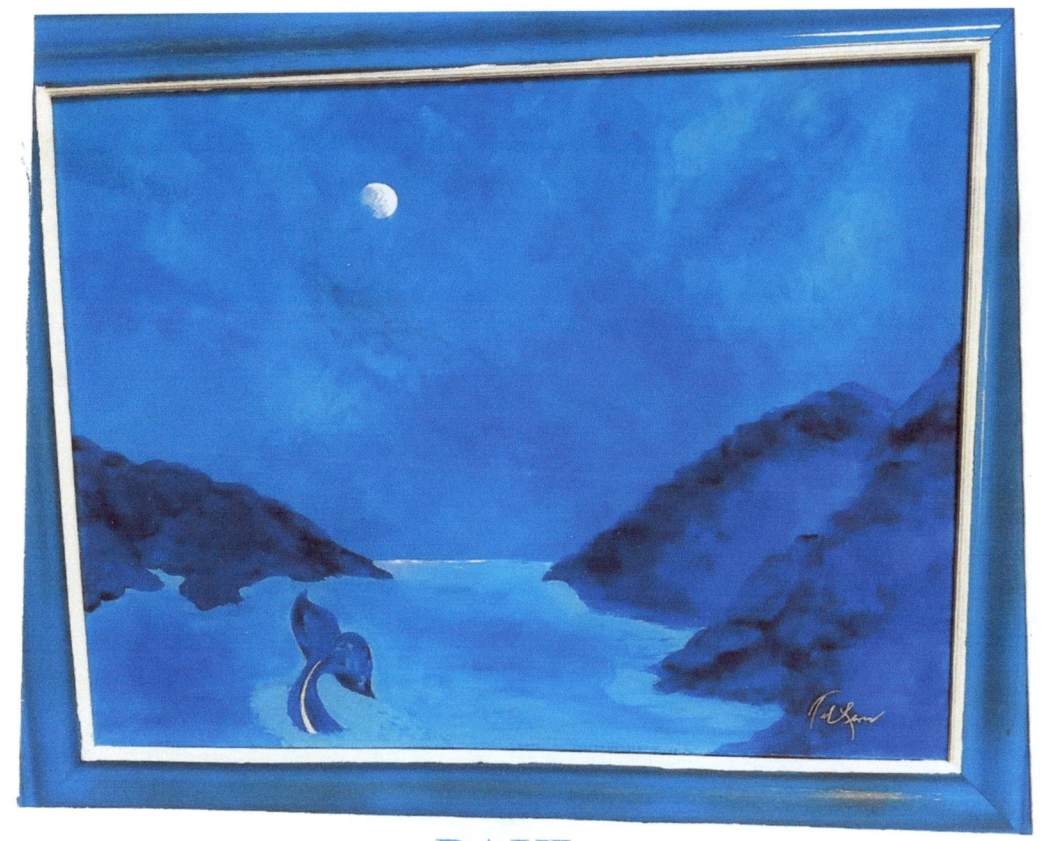

PAUL

THE MIDNIGHT SWIM OF PAUL
THE MAGNIFICENT BULL WHALE
GOING SOUTH FROM THE ALASKAN
COLD ARTIC OCEAN IN SEARCH
OF THE AVAILABLE FEMALE COWS
IN THEIR NATURAL MIGRATION

HE HOPED HE COULD JOIN A POD
FOR THIS 10,000 MILE JOURNEY
ENDING IN THE WARM WATERS
OFF THE COAST OF MEXICO
WHERE THE REAL WHALE ACTION
IN ALL MANORS TOOK PLACE

THE COWS WOULD BE SEEKING
MATES BUT THERE WOULD BE MANY
OF COURSE, THE FEMALES
WERE SELECTIVE FOR ONLY THE BEST
OF THE BULLS WOULD BE CHOOSEN
10 TO 16 MONTHS LATER THE
CALVES WOULD BE BORN

THE MOTHER NURSED AND TAUGHT
THE WAY OF THEIR LIFE AND
SHEILD THEM FROM THE REALITY
OF THE NUMEROUS BABY KILLERS
BECAUSE OF THE POD THE
SHORT FAMILY LIFE WOULD SOON END

IT BECAME TIME TO RETURN
TO THE COLD WATERS OF THE NORTH
THUS, IN KEEPING WITH THEIR
NATURAL INSTINCT AND
A BEAUTIFUL OCEAN WAY OF LIFE
YOU CAN EXPERIENCE THEIR BEAUTY
AT MANY POINTS OF THE JOURNEY

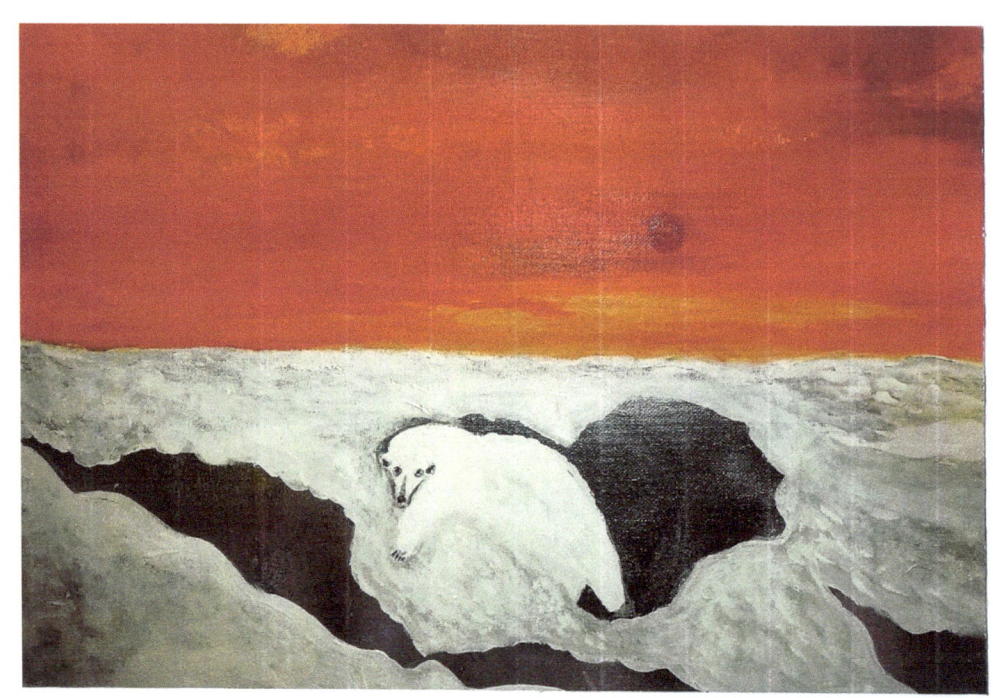

THE FIND
THE LOSS

THE HUNT

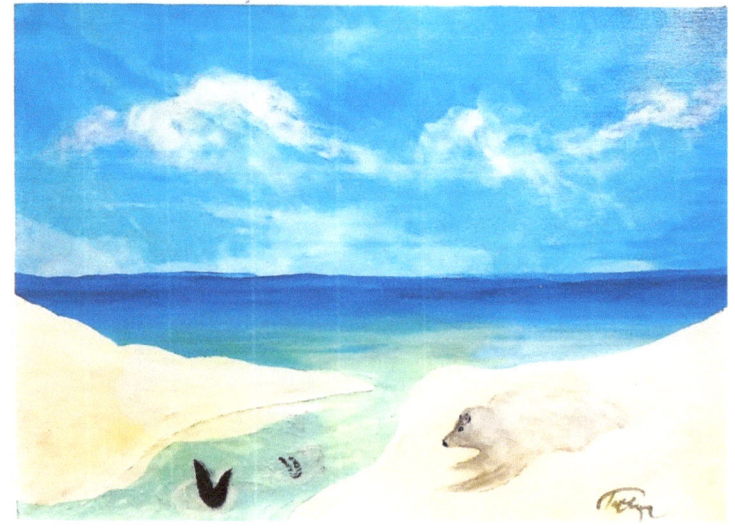

78

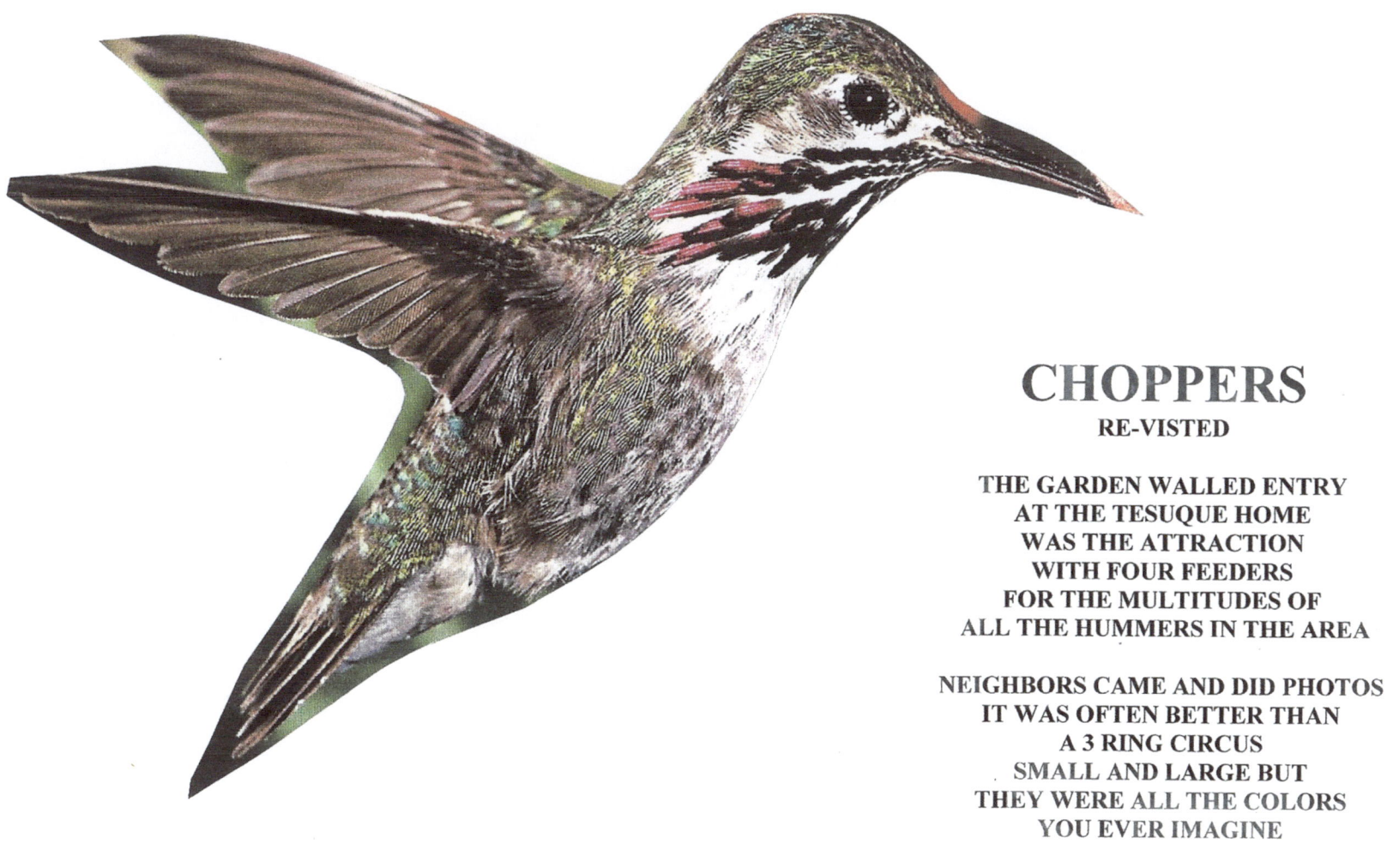

CHOPPERS
RE-VISTED

THE GARDEN WALLED ENTRY
AT THE TESUQUE HOME
WAS THE ATTRACTION
WITH FOUR FEEDERS
FOR THE MULTITUDES OF
ALL THE HUMMERS IN THE AREA

NEIGHBORS CAME AND DID PHOTOS
IT WAS OFTEN BETTER THAN
A 3 RING CIRCUS
SMALL AND LARGE BUT
THEY WERE ALL THE COLORS
YOU EVER IMAGINE

THEY WERE GENTILE AND
SHOWED NO SIGNS OF AGGRESSION
THEY WOULD HOVER AND WAIT
THEIR TURN AT THE FEEDERS
I NEVER HEARD THEM SING
AT MORNING AND TWILIGHT

WITH A ZERO LANDSCAPE
IN MY ALBUQUERQUE TOWNHOUSE
PATIO I ESTABLISED
LA CASTILLO DE LA HUMMERS
SOON THEY CAME IN DROVES
RFILLED FEEDER EVERY 2 DAYS

LARGE AND SMALL
BUT ONLY ONE COLOR
SUBDUED MINT GREEN
WHY NO MULTICOLORS
LIKE THE TESUQUE GARDEN
REASON WHY
I WOULD LIKE TO KNOW

BIG BEHAVIORAL CHANGES
AGRESSION AT THE FEEDERS
FIRST COME IN COMMAND
HIGH PITCHED SONG
SCARED THE OTHERS AWAY
ONE OR TWO CAME BACK

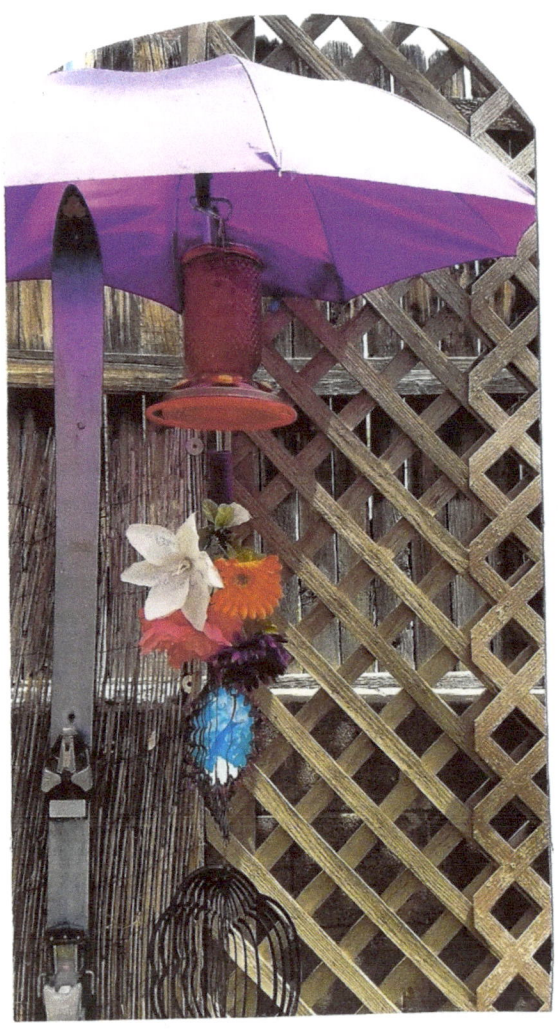

ONLY WHEN THE COMMANDER LEFT
THEN IT WOULD START
ALL OVER AGAIN
SAME COLOR AND BEHAVIOR
AT STEPH'S AND REGINAS

BACK YARD GARDEN HOMES
ALBUQUEQUE HAS MORE FLOWERS
FOR THEM TO FEED
BUT MOST LIKED
THE ONE STOP FEEDER SHOP
THE FLIGHT NATURE
REMAINS THE SAME

THINKING ONLY THE INVIROMENT
CAN PRODUCE THE CHANGE
MAKES SENSE FOR YOU SEE
YOU KNOW IT HAPPENDED
TO YOU AND ME

THEODORO CORONA LUNA

"IT DOESN'T MATTER ANYMORE"

I don't love her anymore

I don't love her anymore

Here's a roll of Jacksons it's all I got

Pack your things I'll send the rest

Get out of my life through the front door

Cabbies waiting tell him where to go

Don't tell me it doesn't matter anymore

Because I don't love you anymore

I slammed the door and had a Lone Star

Three shots of Jack and heated the green chili stew

I known for a while I didn't love her anymore

My heart burst with joy with my new found freedom

To haunt the bars or seek the emerald pebble

Among the many at the beach

To find the gift of new love for the coming years

So it matters that's the only thing I really know

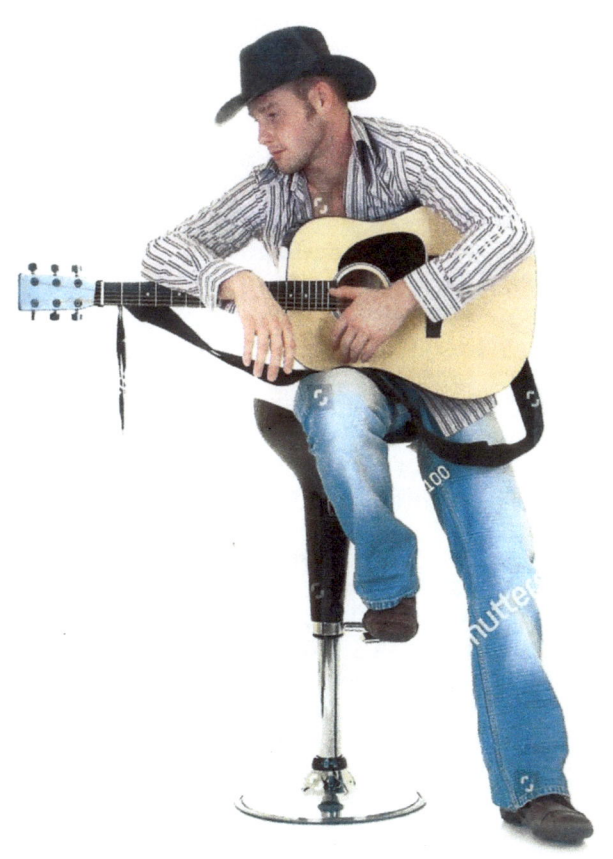

I COMPOSED MY FIRST COUNTRY
MUSIC LYRICS ONLY SONG,
I THOUGHT WILLIE WOULD
ADD THE MUSIC. SENT IT TO HIM
NO RESPONSE. O-WELL, FEEL
FREE TO ADD THE MUSIC
AND PUBLISH, MY CREDIT
IS OPTIONAL

THE FIRST DAM CREATED HERON LAKE
LARGE ENOUGH FOR SMALL SAIL BOATS
SAILING AND REGATAS AND FISHING
WHEN I SAILED MY SMALL FORCE 5
I ALWAYS CAME IN LAST BECAUSE
I COULD NEVER TELL THE WIND
DIRECTION OR WAVE READING

I HAD LEARNED TO SAIL ON THE
COCHITI LAKE CREATED BY THE
LARGEST EARTH DAM IN THE US
FIRST DAY OUT I TURTIED MY F-5
HANGING ON TO THE RUDDER
HYPOTHERMIA STARTED, THE
EARLY SPRING WATER WAS ICE COLD
MY ISTRUCTOR RESCUED ME

THE LAST OF THE MAJOR DAMS
CREATED THE BIG LAKE CALLED
ELEPHANT BUTTE LAKE
LARGER SAIL BOATS AND POWER
BOATS FOR FISHING, WATER
LEVELS VARY PER SEASON

BETWEEN THE LAKES THE RIO
IS OPEN TO ALL SORTS OF
ADVENTURES, SPORTS, FISHING
RAFTING, KAYAKING, SWIMMING
AREAS NAMED BY RAFTING
COMPANIES, TAOS BOX, RACE
COURSE AND MANY OTHERS

MANY SMALL VILLAGES AND
HOMES DOT THE BANKS OF THE RIO
THE NATURAL LANDSCAPES
FROM GRANITE MOUNTAINS TO
PASTORIAL PLANES AND FARMS
INSPIRATIONAL VALLEYS AT
ONE WITH THE INTERNAL SPIRIT

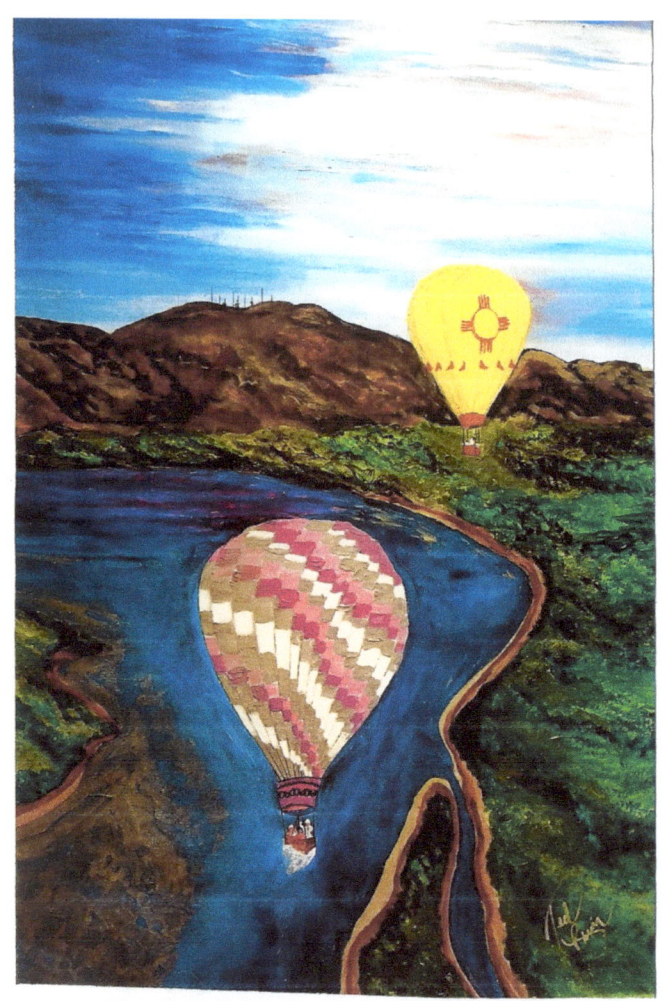

THE KISS ON THE RIO

FARMERS TO THE SOUTH COULD
USE THE WATER ALLOTTED
BY THE MANUAL GATES TO
PLANT THEIR CROPS AND FLOURISH
MANY CROP NAMES EVOLVED SUCH
AS GREEN CHILI FROM HATCH

THE GREAT GRAND MOTHER
RIO GRANDE NURTURES
HER BEST FOR ALL SEASONS
AND FOR ALL HER OWN REASONS
FOR HER LOVE OF NEW MEXICO

LANCE AND LAURA
COLLEGE OF THE UNITED STATES IN THE SOUTHWEST

IN THE MORNING THEY CHECKED THE
RENTAL CAR IN AND ASKED FOR A RIDE
TO MERIDAS AIRPORT KNOWING THE
THE FIRST-CLASS TICKETS WOULD BE THERE
BUT NEVER KNEW TO WHERE THEY WERE
THE DISTINATION WOULD BE

HOLY TAMALE LANCE SAID AS THEY
CHECKED IN, WE ARE HEADED TO
SOUTHWESTERN UNITED STATES
TO A PLACE CALLED ALBUQUERQUE
IN THE STATE OF NEW MEXICO
HE ASKED LAURA HAVE YOU EVER
TRAVELED TO THE WEST
NO, SHE SAID HAVE YOU NO HE SAID

WE BOTH HAVE SPENT OUR EARLY
YEARS ONLY IN THE EASTERN STATES
ABOARD THE PLANE THEY TALKED
ABOUT ALL THE FUN AND WHAT
THEY LEARNED ABOUT THE COLLEGE
OF MEXICO AND WHAT TO DO
WITH THEIR NEARLY FULL
LAP TOPS OF IMAGES AND RECORDINGS

AFTER A VERY SHORT CHAMPAGNE FLIGHT
ARRIVING AT THE SUN PORT
THE LINES AT CUSTOMS WAS SHORT
THE CAR RENTALS WERE AT BAGGAGE CLAIM
THEY CHOOSE AVIS THIS TIME AND
ASKED FOR A ROAD MAP AND BEST HOTEL

THE PRETTY CLERK DID NOT HESITATE
THE BEST IS THE SANDIA RESORT AND CASINO
THEY HAVE EVERY THING AND A GOLF COURSE
WITH THE BEST VEIWS OF THE MOUNTAINS
AND EASY ACCESS TO WHERE YOU WANT TO GO
I'LL MAKE RESERVATIONS FOR YOU

DRIVING UP TO THE HOTEL THEY
IMMEDIATELY LOVED THE SETTING
THE BEAUTIFUL INDIAN LADY AT THE DESK
TOLD THEM WELCOME TO OUR RESERVATION
AND GAVE THEM THE PLASTIC KEY
TO A VERY HIGH-LEVEL SUITE
FACING EAST
TO THE SANDIA MOUNTAINS

LAURA AS SHE SET ON THE SOFA
LANCE THESE ACCOMMODATIONS ARE
FANTASTIC LET'S HAVE AN EARLY DINNER
UP TO TOP RESTAURANT THEY WENT
THEY WERE GREETED AND INFORMED
SIR A COAT IS REQUIRED DON'T WORRY
WE WILL LEND YOU ONE

OVER COCKTAILS AND LATER THEY
ORDERED DINNER AND TALKED
LAURA ASKED LANCE IT HE HAD
EVER GAMBLES HE SIMILED AND
SAID ONLY ONCE AT HARVARD
TELL ME ABOUT IT

MY CURRENT GIRL FRIEND AND
MY ROOM MATE AND HIS GIRL FRIEND
PLAYED STRIP POKER
EVERY ONE WAS DOWN TO THEIR
BIRTHDAY SUITS EXCEPT ME
WITH THE LAST DRAW I LOST
MY REMAING SHORTS, THAT'S IT

HE LOST THEM AGAIN WHEN THEY
WENT TO BED AND LOVED EACH OTHER
EARLY MORNING LANCE SAID
I WANT TO PLAY GOLF AND YOU
CAN GO INTO THE CASINO
THEN WE WILL DO SOME PLANNING

LATER THAT AFTERNOON OVER COCKTAILS
LANCE ASKED LAURA HOW WAS IT
SHE STATED I HAVE NEVER GAMBLED BEFORE
HOW EVER I SOON LEARNED LOST ONLY
ABOUT FIFTY DOLLARS AND HAD FUN
THE COURSE IS BEAUTIFUL FEW TREES
I RECORD MY SCORE OF 104

LOOKING READING ALL THE
STATES BROCHURES AND PAPER ROAD MAP
THAT NEW MEXICO WAS VERY RICH
WITH NATIVE AMERICAN HERITAGE,
SPANISH AND MANY OTHER CULTURES
AND A HOST OF RESERVATION LAND
GIVEN TO THE ORIGINAL INDIAN TRIBES

LAURA WINK AND SMILED ASK LANCE
DO WE NEED A RESERVATION TO SEE
THESE RESERVATIONS? LANCE LAUGHED
OF COURSE, WE DO AS HE WINKED
OK SHE SAID LET'S GO TO SANTA FE
THE CAPTIAL OF THE STATE
AND HEAD QUARTER THERE FOR A WHILE

LAURA SAID I HAVE RESEARCH THE HOTELS
AND THERE ARE MANY IN THE DOWNTOWN AREA
I THINK THE BEST IS THE ELDORADO
IT HAS REAL FIREPLACES AND UNDERGROUND
PARKING WITH VALET SERVICE
SO, I MADE RESERVATIONS, LANCE QUIPPED
WE SURE USE THAT WORD A LOT

AFTER A VERY SHORT 50 MINUTE DRIVE
THEY CHECKED IN AT THE ELDORADO
AS USUAL THEY WERE ESCORTED TO
HIGH FLOOR SUITE WITH A REAL
BEEHIVE FIRE PLACE AND CONTEMPORARY
ADOBE STYLE DECORE WITH ALL
OF THE TRIMMINGS AND WARMTH

LAURA SAID IT'S TO EARLY FOR DINNER
LET'S TAKE A WALK AROUND TOWN
THE FOUND THE CITY SQUARE
KNOWN AS THE PLAZA WITH A
MINI OBELISK IN THE CENTER THEY
SET DOWN ON A GREEN STEEL BENCH
LANCE WITH HIS ARM AROUND LAURA
LET'S REST AND PEOPLE WATCH

THEY COULDN'T GET OVER THE
BLEND OF ALL OF THE DIFFERENT
CULTURES EVEDENT AND OF ALL AGES
AND TOWN FULL OF PEACE AND
THE STORES SEEMED PROSPEROUS
EVEN THOUGH MOST WERE ART GALLERYS

THEY WALKED AROUND A LITTLE MORE
AND THEN WENT BACK TO THE HOTEL
FOR COCKTAILS AND DINNER
THEY KNEW THEY WERE IN A NEW WORLD
BUT LOOKED FORWARD TO THE NEW
ADVENTURE WHERE EVER THEY WOULD GO

AT DINNER LAURA INFORMED LANCE
THEY NEED TO TALK SERIOUSLY
LANCE ASKED WHAT ABOUT
LAURA TOOK A SIP ON HER DRINK
AND LOOKED STRIGHT INTO
LANCE EYES WITH LOVE

LANCE I AM CARRYING OUR CHILD
I NEVER TOLD YOU BEFORE BECAUSE
I HAD TO MAKE SURE AND I AM NOW
LANCE WAS HIT LIKE FALLING STAR
HE HAD TO SORT HIS EMOTIONS
HE'S FIRST WORDS GAME IN DROVES
WITH PURE JOY AS HE KISSED HER

LAURA KISSED HIM BACK
WITH TRUE LOVE AND BOTH
CLINKED THEIR WATER GLASSES
LANCE SAID IT'S TIME TO BE
PRACTICAL AND PLAN WHAT TO DO
WHEN ARE YOU DO FOR THE BIRTH?

IN ABOUT 6 OR 7 MONTHS
PLENTY OF TIME TO PLAN
LAURA ASKED SHOULD WE GET
MARRIED LANCE THOUGHT AND
BECAME SILENT FOR A FEW MINUTES
FIRST, WE SHOULD STAY IN
STATES FOR CITIZENSHIP

SECOND, IF WE DO, WE WILL
HAVE THE STATE OF NEW MEXICO
ENVOLVED IN OUR PRIVATE AFFAIRS
OR WHAT EVER STATE WE MOVE TO
YOU AND I HAVE A COMMENT
TO EACH OTHER BASED ON LOVE
AND A HOST OF OTHER GOOD THINGS

FOR WHAT EVER REASON ONE OF US
SHOULD CHOOSE LEAVE THIS
RELATIONSHIP WHICH I DON'T THINK SO
OUR CHILD WILL BE TAKEN VERY
GOOD CARE OF BECAUSE OF
TRUST FUNDS AND LOVE, WE EACH
KNOW WE BOTH WILL DO OUR BEST

WE CAN AND WILL EXAMINE ALL
OPTIONS IN THE TIME TO COME
BUT RIGHT NOW, WE LOVE
EACH OTHER EVEN MORE
LET'S RETIRE AND HOLD EACH OTHER
IN PEACE AND JOY

WE WILL PLAN TOMARROWS
ADVENTURE AT BREAKFAST
AND LET OUR INTUITIVE NATURE
GUIDE US TO FLOURISH AS WE
DONE IN ALL THE COLLEGES
WE HAVE BEEN IN AND RECORD THIS
NEW WORLD AS WE ALWAYS DO

OVER HEAVOS RANCHEROS
LAURA STATED ITS OVERWHELMING
LANCE SO MANY PLACES TO SEE
VERY CLOSE BY SO LET'S TAKE
A FEW DAYS HERE AND ASK
AROUND FOR A BETTER ITINERARY

THERE ARE ENOUGH INDIAN RESERVATIONS
TO FILL AN EASTERN PROM DANCE CARD
INTERESTING THEY ALL HAVE
DIFFERENT NAMES AND CULTURES
AND MOST OF THEM HAVE MODERNIZED
I THINK WE SHOULD FIND ANCIENT SITES

AFTER A GOOGLE SEARCH LAURA LOOKED
AT LANCE STATING MOST ALL OF THESE
SITES ARE UNDER THE SUPERVISION
OF THE NATIONAL PARK SERVICE
THEY MUST BE NATIONAL TREASURES
I AM SURE THEY ARE LAURA

THE CLOSEST ONE IS BANDELIER
ISN'T IT An ITALIAN NAME I THINK SO
WE COULD START THERE AND THEN
GO TO TAOS TO SEE THEIR PUEBLO
SKIP OVER TO CHACO CANYON
THEN UP TO AZTEC THEN TO COLORADO

NEAR TO THE TOWN OF DURANGO
IS MESA VERDE THEY SAY IT WAS
HOME TO THE ANCIENT ANASAZI
THAT FOUNDED MOST OF THE TRIBES
HERE IN THE SOUTHWEST AS
DESCENDANTS OF THE ANCIENT ONES

I THINK WE CAN FORGET THE REST
EXCEPT FOR BANDELIER SINCE ITS CLOSE
MESA VERDE IS THE PLACE TO GO
JUST BECAUSE I THINK THIS WAS AND IS
THE BIRTH PLACE FOR MANY INDIAN NATIONS
LANCE LUARA AGREED WITH EXCITEMENT

THEY THOROUGHLY ENJOYED ALL ABOUT
THE HISTORY AND INTERESTING RUINS
THEY THROUGHLY ENJOYED THEIR DAY
TRIP TO BANDELIER WITH ITS HISTORY
AND INTERESTING RUINS AND CONCEPTS
OF BUILDING USING WOOD VIGAS WHICH
HOLES OF SUPPORT STILL VISABLE AT
THE CANYONS WALLS AND WAS THE
WOOD THAT CAUSED THE ROOFS
TO CAVE IN AND LEAVING VERY LITTLE
STONE WALLS STANDING

AFTER A WOOD LATTER CLIMB TO
AN OPEN LARGE CAVE WITH A KIVA
THE RANGERS SIGN GAVE A WARNING
"DO NOT THROUGH ROCKS
TO THE CANYON BELOW"
WE LAUGHED BECAUSE WE COULD NOT
FIND ANY AND WONDERED WHO WOULD

OF COURSE, I TOOK A LOT OF IMAGES
LAURA COULD ONLY RECORD THE
RANGER'S TOUR GUIDE STANDARD
VERBIAGE, SHE HAD SPOKEN
IT MANY A THOUSAND TIMES
BACK TO THE ELDORADO WE WENT

AFTER A GOOD NIGHTS REST
AND VERY EARLY IN THE MORNING
WE CHECKED OUT OF THE HOTEL
PAYED OUR NATIONAL DEBT AND
HEADED TO DURANGO COLORADO
JUST A ABOUT A FOUR-HOUR DRIVE
UNLESS THERE WERE TOPES

WE MADE NO HOTEL RESERVATIONS
WE BOTH WANTED TO WING IT
AN OLD LOOKING RED BRICK HOTEL
ON MAIN STREET CAUGHT OUR EYE
JUST ONE SIGN AT THE CORNER
DIAMOND BELLE SALOON
ATTACHED TO THE STRATER HOTEL

THE DESK LADY GAVE US A REAL KEY
TO OUR LARGE CORNER ROOM
ON THE THIRD FLOOR OVERLOOKING
MAIN STREET, SIMPLE TURN OF THE CENTURY
DÉCOR AND PEACEFULLY PLEASING
COCKTAILS WOULD BE AT THE
DIAMOND BELLE SALOON

WE WENT DOWN MAIN STREET
TO THE PALACE RESTAURANT
COMPLETE WITH DART BOARDS
THE WAITER ASKED HOW HUNGRY
WE WERE AND SUGGESTED A DISH
CALLED STEAK Mc MANN
IT WAS A WONDERFUL CULINARY FEAST

NEXT MORNING, WE BOUGHT TICKETS
TO ENTER OUR GOAL, MESA VERDE
LAURA DROVE THE SHORT DISTANCE
WE PARKED AMONG VEHICLES OF TYPES
LOOKING AROUND WE WERE IMPRESSED
HOW WELL THE BUILDINGS AND GROUNDS
WERE DESIGNED INTERGRADED
WITH MUCH CARE TO ITS NATURAL
BEAUTY AND ACCOMMODATIONS
FOR A LARGE NUMBER OF VISTORS

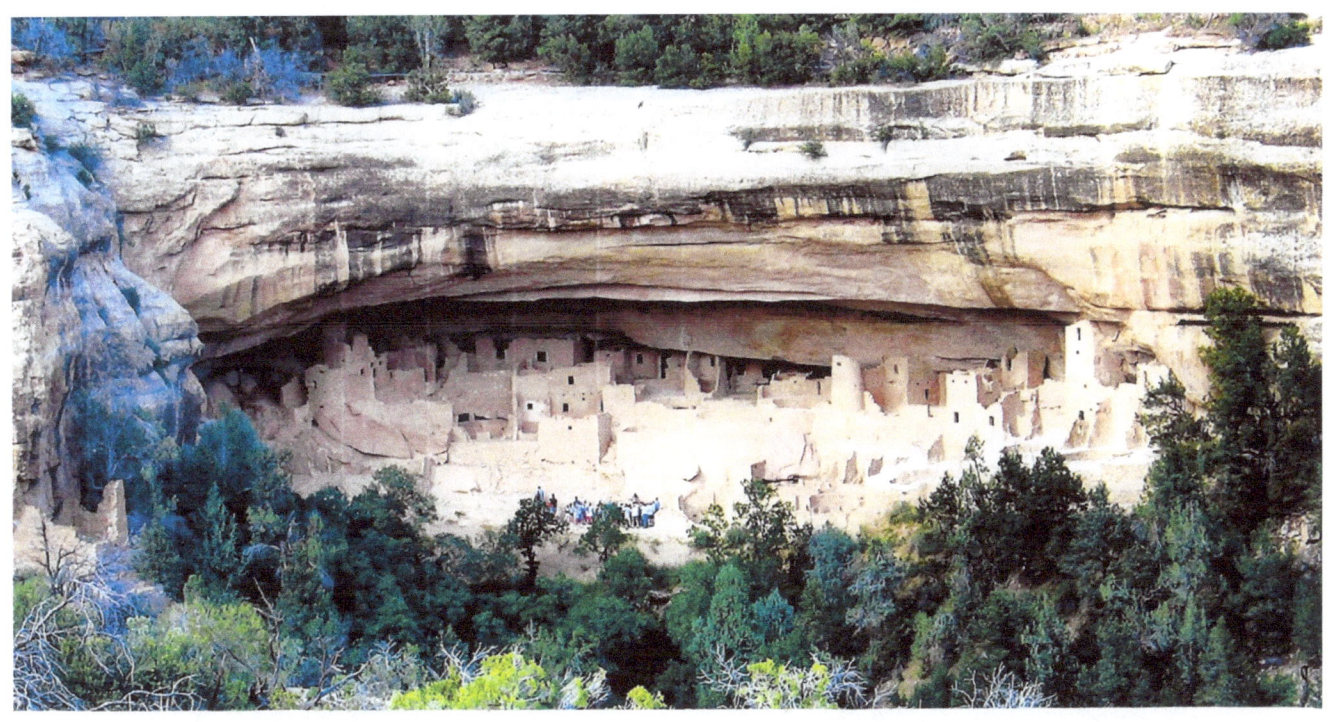

WE HEADED TO THE VISTORS CENTER
WITH IT'S EXHIBIT'S WITH WRITTEN
EXPLANATIONS AND SUGGESTIONS
TO MAKE ANY VIST MEMORABLE
GUIDED TOURS DEPARTED HOURLY
WITH VERY MINABLE FEES

I TOLD LAURA THIS TOUR WAS
THE BEST WAY TO GET AN OVERVIEW
I FELT IT WAS IMPOSSIBLE TO
VIST THE ENTIRE SITE IN ONE DAY
SHE SAID LET'S TAKE THE TOUR TODAY
OVER NIGHT SOME WHERE AND COME
BACK TOMORROW

IT BECAME A JAW DROPPING AWE
EXPERIENCE, WHO WOULD HAVE EVER
THOUGHT TO BUILD AND ENTIRE VILLAGE
IN A VERY LARGE OPEN-END CAVE
THE TOUR GUIDE EXPLAINED THE
ANCIENT FORCES THAT MADE IT
AN NATURAL SOLUTION FOR THE
ANCIENT ANASAZI

I COMMENTED TO THE PRETTY GUIDE
HOW WONDERFUL THE WEATHER WAS?
IT'S BECAUSE OF THE START OF
INDIAN SUMMER, PLEASE EXPLAIN
IT IS THE TIME BEFORE FALL WITH
DAYS WARM AND NIGHTS COLD

THE VILLAGE ARCHITECTURE WAS
NATURAL AND FLOWING IN GRACE
THE STONE WORK IMPECCABLE AND
AS NEEDED THE CLOSE FOREST
PROVIDED ANY WOOD TIMBER FOR ROOFS
AND OF COURSE, FOR FIRES THE
VALLEY WAS FARMED, I SURE
THE ANCIENT ONES HAD A GOOD LIFE

LATE IN THE TOUR I SLOWED DOWN
AND LET THE GROUP GET FAR AHEAD
OF ME, LAURA WAS WITH THEM
I CIRCLED BACK AND CLIMBED INTO
ONE OF THE HIGH ROOFS LESS ROOMS
AND SET DOWN TO REST

LEANED MY BACK AGAINST THE STONE
WALL AND HAD A DRINK OF WATER
CLOSED MY EYES THEN OPENED THEM
TO A WHITE BRIGHT LIGHT IN THE
MIDDLE OF THE ROOM SOON IT
BECAME DIM AND AN ABERRATION
APPEARED AND BEGAN TO TAKE FORM

AS IT MATERIALZED AN OLD MAN
WITH LONG BRAIDED WHITE HAIR
WEATHERED FACE WITH SAD
BROWN EYES WAS WRAPPED IN
A LONG COLORFUL BLANKET HE
LOOKED STRIAGHT AT ME

HAVE NO FEAR I AM TO YOU A FRIEND
MY SPIRIT HAS TRAVEL THIS LAND
SO, I WAS ABLE TO LEARN THE
WHITE MANS WORDS WHICH I CAN
SPEAK TO YOU, BECAUSE OUR
ANCIENT WORDS WOULD HAVE NO
MEANING AND UNDERSTANDING

I CHOOSE YOU BECAUSE I KNEW
YOU ARE A MAN OF TRUTH AND
HAVE A VERY SPECIAL GIFT
CALLED TELEPATHIC POWERS
I AM AN ANCIENT ANASAZI HISTORIAN
JUST CALL ME THE ANCIENT ONE
HE NEVER ASKED ME MINE

THE TRUTHS AND LEGENDS
WILL UNFOLD AS I SPEAK NOTHING
WAS EVERY WRITTEN IN ANY FORM
JUST AS YOU SAY WORD OF MOUTH
GENERATION AFTER GENERATION
THE LENGTH OF OUR LIVES WAS
NUMBERED BY THE SEASONS

LEGEND FROM OUR GREAT GRANDFATHERS
THAT IN THE BEGINNING THEY CROSS A
NARROW BRIDGE FROM A FAR-OFF LAND
AND FOUND THE NEW LAND TO COLD
THE LEADERS LEAD THE PEOPLE SOUTH
MANY DEFECTED AND STARTED THERE
NEW TRIBES THAT WERE SCATTERED
IN AREAS THEY COULD PROSPER

IT WAS A VERY LONG AND ARDUOUS JOURNEY
AS IT BECAME WARMER AND THE LAND
COULD SUPPORT LIFE MANY STOPPED
AND FORMED THEIR OWN CULTURE
STILL MANY HEADED SOUTH AND
WE HAD NO NAME FOR OUR NEW LANDS

OUR GREAT, GREAT GRANDFATHERS
FOUND THE LAND WHERE THE PLAINS
HAD CREATURES TO EAT AND
WATER BOUNDING WITH PLANTS
IN SEASON TO NOURISH AND
SOON WE LEARNED HOW TO FARM

AT THAT TIME WE HAD NO WARRING TRIBES
BUT OUR SCOUTS DISCOVER A LARGE
NATURAL CAVE WHICH WAS A SHELTER
FROM THE SEASONS WITH A CANYON
BELOW WITH WATER AND A FOREST
WE NAMED THIS PLACE AND OUR PEOPLE
THE ANASAZI WE CREATED A FUTURE
LEGACY THAT WOULD CREAT DESTING

GENERATIONS AFTER GENERATIONS
OUR YOUNG ONES HEADED FURTHER
SOUTH AND CLAIMED THEIR LAND
WITH NEW NAMES FOR THEIR TRIBES
IN ROAMING IN SPIRIT, I NEW THEY
FLOURISHED NEVER TO THIS DAY
THEY DON'T FORGET TO HONOR
US AS THE ANASAZI GRANDFATHERS
THE ANCIENT ONES

THE ANCIENT ONE GREW TIRED
AND SOON HE STARTED TO DISSOLVE
I NEW MY CAMERA WAS USELESS
IT WOULD NOT CAPTURE THE IMAGE
OF A SPIRIT AND I TRIED TO SHAKE
HIS HAND NOTHING WAS THERE
THEN I HEARD HIS LAST WORDS TO ME
"LANCE CONTINUE YOUR PATH"
THEN HE WAS GONE, I WAS ALONE AGAIN

I NEEDED A STRONG DRINK BUT
ALL I HAD WAS BOTTLED WATER
HOW I WISHED THAT LAURA WAS
HERE TO RECORD WHAT GIFT
WAS JUST GIVEN TO ME, BUT
I KNEW THIS WOULD HAVE NEVER
HAPPENED IF SHE WAS HERE

I WAS BLESSED WITH A VERY GOOD
MEMORY AND I WOULD RECITE THE
STOREY FULLY FOR HER RECORDER
DOWN THE PATH I WENT AND
SOON REJOINED THE GROUP
LAURA LOOKED AT ME AND
SAID LANCE YOU WEREN'T GONE LONG

I SIMILED AND SAID "I JUST TOOK
A REST AND DO I HAVE A STOREY
TO TELL YOU TONIGHT"
I THINK I KNOW WHAT IT MIGHT
BE I WON'T BE SURPRISED
ARM IN ARM AFTER THE TOUR
ENDED WE HEADED TO THE CAR

FINDING A CLOSE MOTEL AND IT
HAD A RESTAURANT, THEY HAD
A FAST COCKTAIL AND DINNER
WENT BACK TO THEIR SPARTAN ROOM
SITTING ON THEIR BED LAURA
TOOK OUT HER RECORDER
AND TOLD LANCE TO GO FOR IT

IT TOOK TWO FULL BLANK TAPES
TO RECORD LANCE'S STOREY
LAURA SET WIDE EYED AND STUNNED
FINALLY, SHE SPOKE IN JOY
LANCE THAT'S THE BEST STOREY
OF OUR TRIPS, WOW
OVER THE SECOND CUP OF COFFEE
AT BREAKFAST, LAURA WE HAVE
DONE EVERYTHING WE CAME FOR
AT MESA VERDE, LET'S HEAD
BACK TO DURANGO AND GO
BACK TO SANTA FE, WE CAN TALK
ABOUT THINGS IN THE CAR

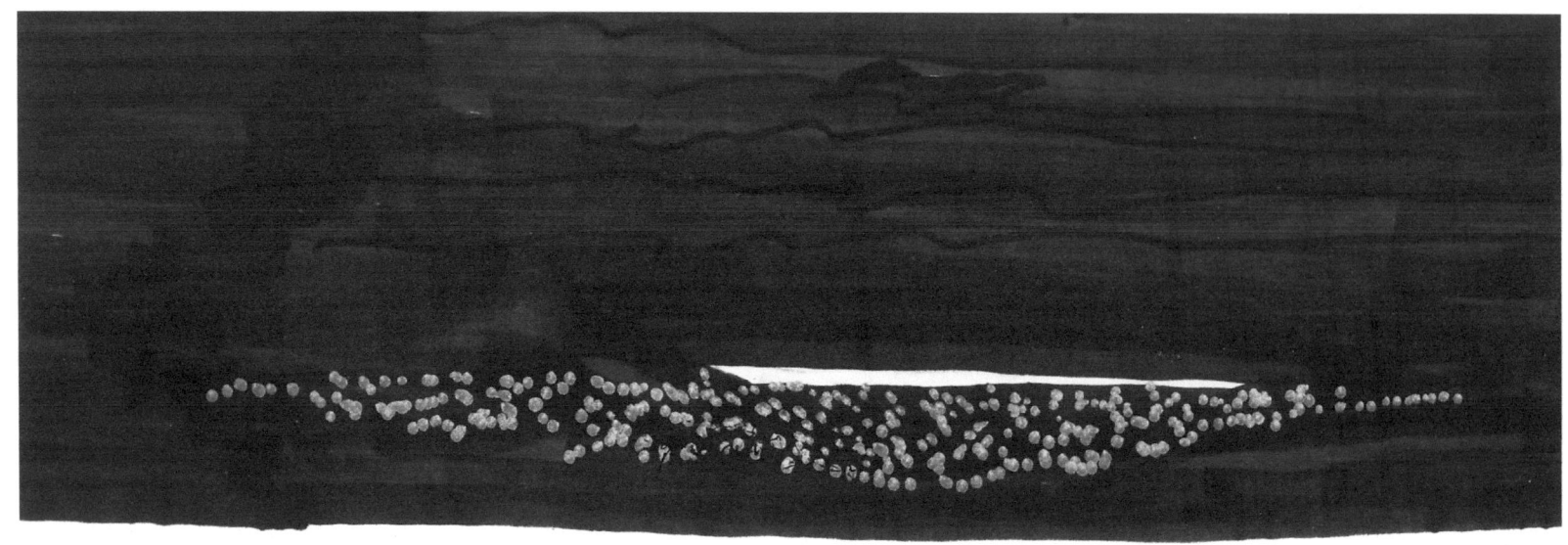

DIAMONDS AND YOU
A LOVE STOREY

ON HIGH MOUNTAIN ROAD
LATE AT NIGHT STARS WINKLE
NO MOON IN SIGHT
WE STOPPED TO REST AND
LOOKED AT THE VALLEY BELOW

A SEA OF DIAMONDS SPARKLED
FROM THE LARGE CITY LIGHTS BELOW
SHE SHARED HER THOUGHTS
SPOKE IN SWEET TONES
CLOSE YOUR EYES AND HOLD MY HAND

NATURE'S MOST PRECIOUS GIFT
IS RARE AND GRAND LIKE YOU
YOU ARE A DIAMOND
WHO HAS CRYSTALLIZED?
THROUGH CREATION AND
THRUST UPWARD TO BECKON LIFE

AN UNCONQUERABLE SPIRIT
WHOSE FLAME OF LOVE REFLECTS
THE ETERNITY OF THE UNIVERSE
KNOWLEDGE OF LIFE
YOU ARE ADAMAS GIFT OF LOVE
LIKE A DIAMOND MORE EVEN
PRECIOUS WITH TIME

CLARITY WITHOUT INCLUSIONS
REFLECTING COLORS WITHIN OUR WORLD
CREATED BY THE UNIVERSE
AND CUT BY MANS HAND
BEAUTY UNSERPASSED KNOWN TO ALL
YOU ARE A PART OF THE SEA
OF DIAMONDS RARE AND PRECIOUS

YOUR SPIRIT WILL BE FED
WITH MANY MOMENTS OF RICHNESS
BEHOLD THE GLORY
THAT ONLY YOU AND I CAN CLAIM
GROW IN LOVE AND WE WILL
CREATE OUR OWN
SEA OF DIAMONDS

I OPENED MY EYES WITH A TEAR OR TWO
I NEW MY LOVE FOR HER WAS OVER
SAD BUT TRUE BUT I KNEW WHAT TO DO
MY WORDS CAME SLOW
IT WOULD HURT HER AND TEARS
OF EMOTIONAL FEELINGS WOULD
FLOOD THE CAR AS I SAID

LIKE THE WILD WINDS WITH SNOW
IT'S COOL AND FLAKES CUDDLE
OUR SEPARATE SPIRITS FLOATS
THEN TURNS TO PUDDLES

THEODORO CORONA LUNA
FOR AND PARTS BY CINDY
A VERY SHORT SCOTTSDALE LOVE

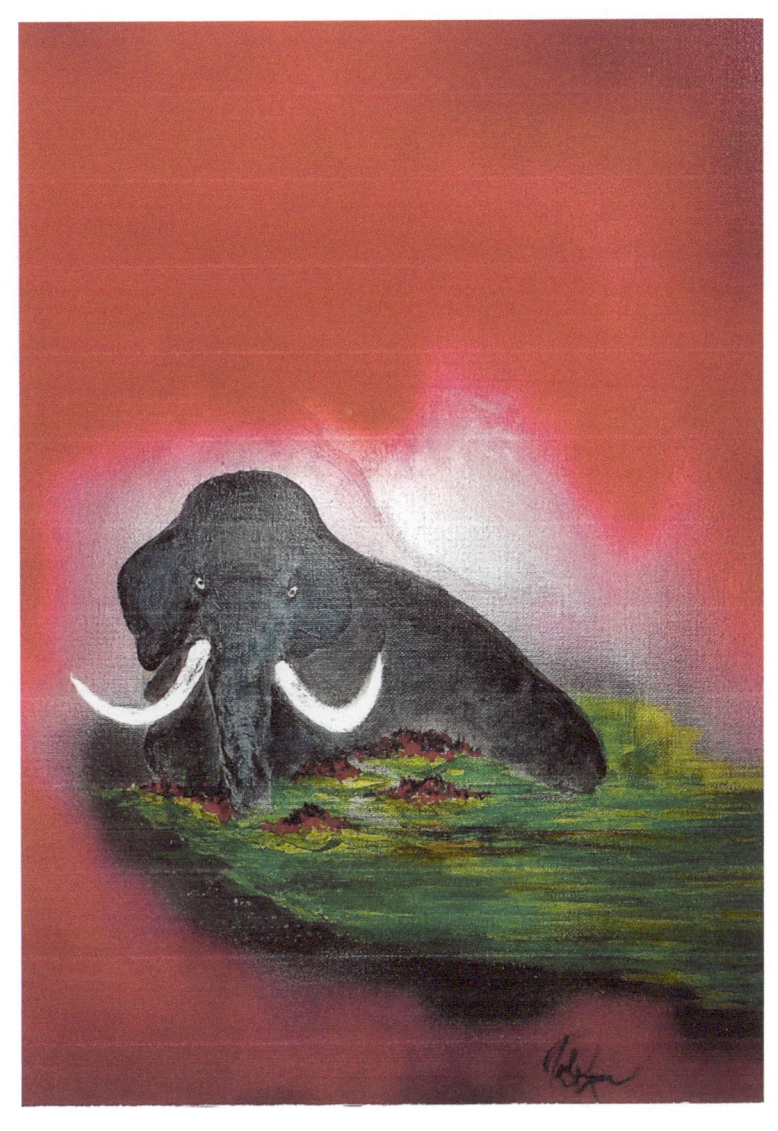

"I FOUND COOL, COOL WATER"

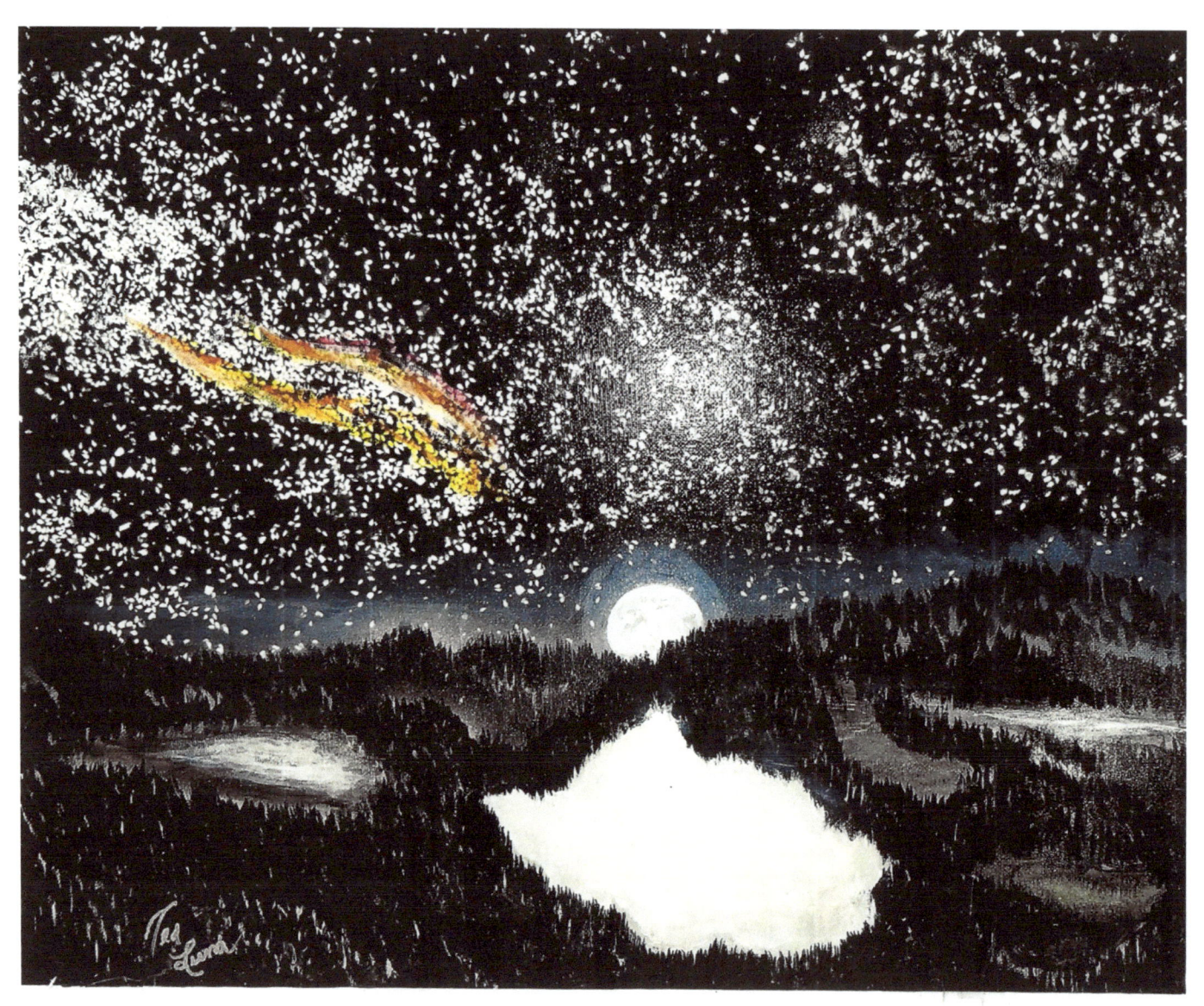

"MY STARRY NIGHT"

LANCE & LAURA
BACK TO SANTA FE

BACK AT THE STRATER EARLY
BOTH TOOK AN AFTERNOON NAP
REFREASHED THEY HAD COCKTAILS
AT THE BELLE AND WENT TO DINNER
AT THE ORE HOUSE FOR DINNER
KING CRAB LEGS HERE IN DURANGO

BEFORE BED LANCE ASKED LUARA
TO MAKE RESERVATIONS FOR A HOTEL
IN SANTA FE, AFTER A GOOGLE SEARCH
SHE MADE A CALL AND PROUDLY
ANNOUNCED LANCE ARE YOU SETTING
DOWN WE HAVE RESERVATIONS
AT THE INN OF THE ANASAZI
I HOPE THE ANCIENT ONE IS THERE

DURING THE DRIVE LANCE
NEW IT WAS TIME OFFER SOME
THINGS HE HAD THOUGHT ABOUT
LAURA. WE NEED TO SETTLE DOWN
FOR A WHILE FOR YOU AND
OUR BABYS SAKE AND I KNOW
WE BOTH LIKE SANTA FE

. LET'S EXPLORE THE POSSIBILITIES
SETTLED AT THE INN AND DURING
THEIR FIRST DINNER THEIR, LANCE SAID
I THINK WE SHOULD BUY A HOME
SOME PLACE JUST OUT SIDE OF THE CITY
THE COUNTRY SIDE IS PEACEFUL AND
LOTS OF TREES CALLED PINON

NEXT MORNING, THEY SEARCH
AND CALLED A REALITOR BY THE
TOSS OF A COIN THERE WERE MANY
SHE ANSWERED ON THE SECOND RING
AND OFFERED TO MEET THEM IIN
THE LOBBY TO DISCUSS THEY NEEDS

OVER A DRINK THEY BONDED
I THINK THE AREA BEST SUITED
TO LOOK IS TESUQUE, LOTS OF LISTINGS
ITS JUST OVER THE NORTH HILL
AND IN A VALLEY, LANCE SMILED
I REMEMBER THE SIGN ON THE HIGHWAY
A LOT OF MOVIES STARS BUY AND LEAVE
IN A FEW YEARS, I GUESS THEY MISS
WHAT MADE THEM STARS BUT MOST
OF THEIR HOMES ARE BEAUTIFUL
AND PRICED ON THE GOING MARKET

LITTLE DID SHE KNOW THE DEEP
POCKETS OF LANCE AND LAURA
WE CAN MEET IN THE MORNING
TO SHOW YOU SOME OF THE BEST
LISTINGS AND I'LL DRIVE MOST
OF THEM ARE GATED FOR PRIVACY

SHE SHOWED UP DOUBLED PARKED
AT THE FRONT DOOR IN HER NEW
RED 4 WHEEL FORD SUV WITH
TRAVELING INSULATED CUPS
OF COFFEE AND DOUGHNUTS
LANCE AND LAURA CLIMB IN

THE MORNING WAS LIKE A WHIRLWIND
OF VEIWING MANY HOMES AND
FEW INTERIOR VISITATIONS
SHE TOOK THEM FOR LUNCH
AT THE TESUQUE VILLAGE MARKET
BEER AND RED CHILI ENCHILADAS

I THINK YOUR BOTH READY TO
SEE THE OLDEST AND BEST DEVELOPMENT
SANGRE DECRISTO ESTATES ONLY
ONE LISTING THERE BUT A NICE ONE
ITS EMPTY AND I HAVE THE KEYS
I HOPE IT WILL MEET YOUR NEEDS

YOU WILL HAVE SHORT AND EASY
ACCESS TO THE OPERA NATIONALLY
ACCLAMED, TESUQUE MARKET AND
ABOUT 10 MINUTES TO ALBERTSON
FOR ALL OF YOUR DOMESTIC NEEDS
ITS ORINTATION HAS THE BEST VIEWS
OF THE MOUNTAINS AND ITS GATED

LANCE YOU MENTIONED YOU PLAY GOLF
THE BUFFALO THUNDER RESORT AND
CASINO HAS ONE TOWA ITS ONLY
15 MINUTES NORTH AND BLACK MESA
IS JUST SOUTH OF ESPANOLA
LANCE THOUGHT THE INDIANS
SURE, HAVE A LOT OF CASINOS

THEY ALSO HAVE A HOME OWNERS
ASSOCIATION OF NICE PEOPLE WHO
ONLY LEAVE WHEN THEY DIE AND
NO REQUIREMENTS FOR NEW OWNERS
THEY TAKE GOOD CARE OF THEIR
ROADS, WATER AND MUTUAL INTERESTS

THE ADDRESS FOR THIS HOME IS
NUMBER FOUR SANGRE DECRISTO ESTATES
EVEN THOUGH IT'S THE FIRST HOUSE
ON THE RIGHT AFTER THE GATE
IT WAS DESIGNED AND BUILT BY
AN ARCHITECT NAMED TED LUNA
HE LIVED THERE 13 YEARS, LANCE
LOOKED AT LAURA IS THIS THE
TED, WE KNOW, HE NEVER TOLD US
OR MENTIONED HIS LAST NAME

DRIVING UP TO ESTATES LAURA
THERE IS ANOTHER GATE FOR
TESUQUE HILLS ITS NICE TOO
BUT THERE ARE NO LISTINGS THERE
IT WAS LATER DONE BY THE
SAME DEVELOPER OF THE ESTATES
THEY PARKED THE SUV AT
THE WALLED ENTRY GATES

BEFORE WE GO IN, I WOULD LIKE
TO TELL YOU ABOUT THE PREVIOUS
OWNER AND WHY ITS ON THE MARKET
HE AND HIS WIFE LIVED HERE
MANY YEARS TILL THE DIVORCE
SHE LEFT AND HE KEPT THE HOUSE

A FEW MONTHS LATER HE MET
THE LOVE OF HIS LIFE AT THE
PALACE BAR SHE WAS EASTERN WEALTHY
TAKED HIM TO GO WITH HER BACK EAST
HE LEFT ALL HIS AFFAIRS WITH AN
ATTORNEY NAMED RON VAN AMBERG
IN SANTA FE WITH FULL POWER
OF ATTORNEY RIGHTS INCLUDING
ALL AFFAIRS AND HOUSE

SHE OPENED THE GATES AND
MENTIONED THE 4 ACRES INCLUDED
THE WALK THROUGH THE GARDEN
ENTRY AND TO THE FRONT DOOR
LAURA ASK WHY THE METAL ROOFS
AND MULTIPLE DORMORES AND
MOST OF ALL THE PITCHED ROOFS
THE ARCHITECT WANTED A CONTEMPORY
EXPRESSION OF INDIGENES' NORTHERN
NEW MEXICO ARCHITECTURE
LANCE COMMENTED I CAN'T WAIT
TO GO INSIDE LAURA AGREED

THEY WERE BOTH OVERWHELM AT
OPEN SPACES AND LOVED THE
MULTILEVELS ESPECIALLY THE
OPEN MASTER SUITE ON THE OPEN
SECOND FLOOR OVERLOOKING
ALL OF THE SPACES BELOW
AND THE OLD FASHION BATH TUB

UP TO THE LARGE OPEN STUDIO
OVER THE GARAGE THRU DOORS
FOR PRIVACY AND BATH WITH
ACCESS ALSO THROUGH THE DOUBLE
DOOR LARGE GARAGE, ALL YOU
NEED IS BED FOR GUESTS
LANCE THOUGHT IF THE
ANCIENT ONE VISTS US WE
WOUN'T NEED A BED

IT'S PERFECT FOR OUR NEEDS
A GREAT PLACE TO WORK WITH
MY PHOTOGRAPHY AND YOU
TO WRITE YOUR BOOKS LAURA
AND NURTURE OUR BABY
YOU TWO NEED TO TALK AND
I'LL WAIT FOR YOU DOWNSTAIRS

THEY WENT BACK DOWN AND
ASKED THE PRICE IT WAS LISTED FOR
THE LADY TOLD THEM BUT THEY
COULD MAKE AN OFFER
LANCE LOOKED AT LAURA AND SAID
I THINK WE SHOULD SPLIT IT
THEN WE BOTH OWN IT
LAURA HARDLY AGREED

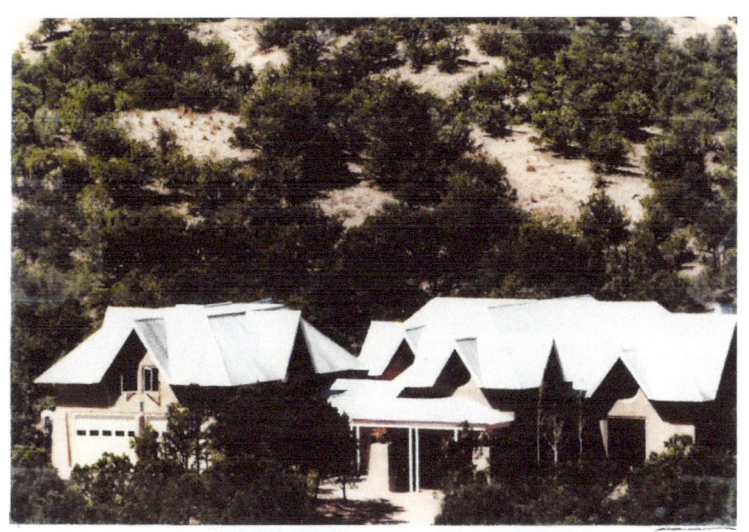

LANCE TOLD THE LADY WE
WILL TAKE IT AT THAT PRICE
HOW SOON CAN WE CLOSE
SHE SAID AS SOON AS THE FUNDS
CLEAR THE BANK RON WILL
SIGN IT OVER SINCE THE TITLE
IS CRYSTAL CLEAR

IN RONS OFFICE THE NEXT MORNING
ALL TRANSACTIONS WENT SO FAST
THE NEVER HAD A SECOND CUP OF
COFFEE THE FUNDS CLEARED FASTER
THEN LIGHTING IN A DARK SKY
LANCE ASKED RON IF HE KNEW
AND INTERIOR DECORATOR THAT
COULD LOCALLY FURNISH THE HOUSE

RON SMILED AND GAVE HIM THE
NAME AND NUMBER AND ADDED
SHE IS THE BEST AROUND AND
CALL HER AND SEE IF SHES FREE
FOR SERVICES NOT FOR FEE
LANCE AND LAURA LAUGHED

NEXT EARLY MORNING THE ID
LADY NAMED EMBER VAN BEHN MET THEM
FOR COFFEE AT THE HOTEL AND
AFTER A GOOD GET AQUITENANCE
SHE SAID THEY COULD CALL HER EM
THEY CLIMB IN TO HER WHITE SUV
LAURA TOLD LANACE WE NEED TO
BUY A SUV YOU PICK THE COLOR

EM WAS DELIGHTED WITH THE HOUSE
SHE TOOK NOTES ON THEIR NEEDS
AND SUGGESTED A FEW IDEAS
WHEN THEY WERE DONE, THEY
SET ON THE STAIRS AND LANCE
ASK EM HOW FAST COULD THIS BE DONE

EM SMILED AND SAID ABOUT A YEAR
HOWEVER, I CAN DO IT IN TWO WEEKS
THEY ALL AGREED ON HER FEE
YOU CAN PAY ON SATISFACTION
WHEN EVERY THINGS IN PLACE
GO FOR IT AND HERE IS OUR
CELL PHONE NUMBER TO CONTACT US

THEY WENT SUV SHOPPING
LAURA TOLD LANCE WE SHOULD
BUY AMERICAN NOT FOREIGN TO
WELCOME US BACK TO THE STATES
FORD WON OUT AND INSTOCK
WAS A GOLD COLORED BEAUTY
HAD EVERY THING INCLUDING
A PICTURE OF A KITCHEN SINK

THOUGH THE NEXT DAYS THAT
FOLLOWED THEY TRIED TO BE
AT THE HOUSE WHEN DELIVERYS
WERE MADE AND LOVED THE
FURNISHINGS THAT WERE MAKING
THE HOUSE THEIR HOME
IT SOON WAS TOTALLY FINISHED
AND DECIDED TO HAVE A
HOUSE WARMING CELEBRATION
HOPING THE ANCIENT ONE
WOULD COME

THEY SOON SETTLED IN AND WENT
SHOPPING FOR CLOTHES AND ALL
THE THINGS THEY NEEDED WHICH
WAS FUN WITH THE SEASONS
WEATHER IN MIND IN THE PAST
IT WAS JUST A CARRY-ON
SOME HOW THEY FELT SETTLED

THEIR WORK IN THE STUDIO BLOSSOMED
IT DID NOT FEEL LIKE WORK
IT WAS JOYFUL AND PRODUCTIVE
AS LUARA'S BOOKS DEVELOPED
LANCE LET LAURA INCLUDE
ANY OF THE IMAGES HE HAD TAKEN

THE HAD BOUGHT STATE OF THE ART
COMPUTERS, LANCE MADE CONTACT
WITH HIS NATIONAL FRIENDS THAT
WOULD PUBLISH THE IMAGES HE
SELECTED FOR APPROPRIATE FEES
LAURA SCANNED FOR PUBLISHERS

LAURA WAS GETTING LARGER
WITH THE BABY SOON DUE
THE HOSPITAL SCANS WERE POSITIVE
FOR IT WAS TO BE A GIRL
THEY BOTH HAD FUN IN TRYING
TO SELECT A NAME

VERY LATE FALL AND EARLY WINTER
LAURA TOLD LANCE WE ARE ABOUT
3 WEEKS OF MY DUE DATE IT
COULD BE ANY TIME NOW
LATE ONE NIGHT LAURA WOKE
LANCE SHE WAS IN PAIN
TIME TO GO TO THE HOSPITAL

THE FAST TRIP TO ST. VINCENTS
RIGHT UP TO THE ER ENTRANCE
THEY HELPED LAURA INTO A GURNEY
LANCE PARKED THE SUV AND RACED
BACK TO THE ER ENTRANCE
HE WAS INFORMED THAT THEY
HAD TAKEN LUARA TO DELIVERY

HE WAS GIVEN DIRECTIONS AND
WOULD BE ALLOWED IN TO BE
WITH LAURA WHEN HE OPENED
THE DOOR THE DOCTORS AND
NURSES WERE ATTENDING HER
SHE WAS SCREAMING IN PAIN

THEY PUT A SMOCK ON HIM
HE WENT TO LAURA AND KISSED
ON HER FORHEAD AND HELD
HER HAND AND SPOKE REASURING
TO CALM HER THE BEST HE COULD
HER WATER HAD BROKEN IN THE SUV

BOTH DOCTORS HELP TO DELIVER
THE BABY ONE TOOK THE BABY AWAY
FROM VIEW AND DID THINGS
TO MAKE THE BABY BREATH AND
CRY HE DID HIS VERY BEST THEN
HANDED THE BABY TO A NURSE

HE WALKED BACK TO LAURA AND
LANCE WITH A VERY SAD ALMOST
TEARFUL LOOK AND SAID
I DID EVERY THING I COULD
THE BABY WAS STILLBIRTH.

BOTH LAURA AND LANCE
STARTED CRYING THE DOCTOR
PUT HIS ARMS AROUND THEM
AND FELT A TEAR IN HIS EYES
WE WILL KEEP LAURA OVER NIGHT
LANCE YOU CAN STAY ALSO

THEIR SORROW WAS TO DEEP
FOR SLEEP THEY MANAGED TO
COMFORT EACH OTHER THE
BEST THEY COULD TILL MORNING
SUN FLOODED THE ROOM
LET'S GIVE THE BABY A PROPER
BURIAL AND THEY DID

BACK AT THEIR HOME
THEY WERE TRYING TO ASSIMILATE
THE TRAGEDY OF THE ORDEAL
EACH KNEW IT WOULD TAKE A WHILE
LAURA IN TIME TO COME
WE CAN TRY AGAIN THIS
WAS THE FIRST TIME LAURA SMILED

LANCE TOLD LAURA I DON'T
KNOW WHAT THE FUTURE
MAY BRING US BUT WE BOTH
LOVE TESUQUE AND ARE HOME
IF WE TRAVEL, WE CAN ALWAYS
HAVE A HOUSE SITTER
AND COME HOME

LAURA ASKED LANCE
WHERE DO YOU THINK
TED WILL SEND US NEXT
I DON'T KNOW
IT PROBABLY DEPENDS
IF TED WANTS TO WRITE
HIS FOURTH BOOK

THE WHITE HOUSE

WASHINGTON

June 13, 2019

Dear Mr. Luna, Architect,

Thank you for your letter and thoughtful gesture.

As President, I am honored to serve our Nation. The United States is made great by millions of talented individuals who use their time, skills, and resources to help improve their communities and the lives of their fellow Americans. Together, we will continue to build a stronger, safer, and more prosperous country.

Melania and I send our best wishes.

Sincerely,

[signature]

THIS WAS MY RESPONSE FROM THE WHITE HOUSE.
30 DAYS LATER WHEN I E-MAILED A VERY DETAILED
RESTORATION CONCEPT FOR DONALD TO SEND
TO THE PRESIDENT OF FRANCE FOR A FAST METHOD
OF RECONSTRUCTION AT NOTRE DAME. I THINK THAT
THE FIRE WAS STARTED BY A WORKERS CIGARETTE
DROPING INTO AN ANCIENT BEEHIVE AT QUITING
TIME. IN LIEU OF WOOD TRUSSES, STEEL A-FRAMED
FOR FAST ERECTION AND SO MANY OTHER DETAILS.
I CAN ONLY SURMISE DONALD NEVER SO IT. THE
WHITE HOUSE FILTER SYSTEM AT ITS BEST.

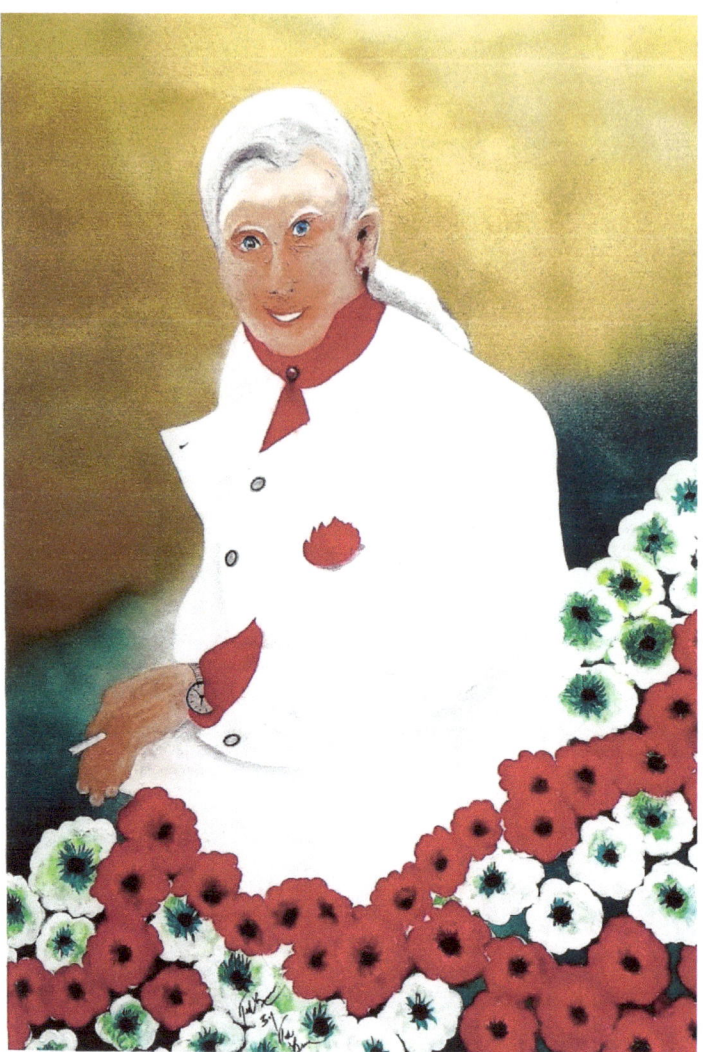

I KNOW WHERE I'VE BEEN,   I KNOW WHERE I'M AT
I KNOW I MUST GO,   ON MY JOURNEY UNKNOWN

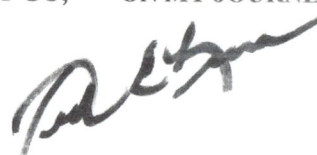